GOD'S
REVELATION
AND
YOUR FUTURE

SALVATION TRUTH AS
REVEALED FROM THE
BOOK OF REVELATION

W0010966

GOD'S REVELATION AND YOUR FUTURE

Tim R. Barker, D. Min.

*Superintendent of the South Texas
District of the Assemblies of God*

Tim R. Barker Ministries

GOD'S REVELATION AND YOUR FUTURE, Barker, Tim.
1st ed.

Formatting, proofing, and cover provided by:
Farley Dunn
of
Three Skillet Publishing
⬤⬤⬤ THREE SKILLET
www.ThreeSkilletPublishing.com

Tim R. Barker Ministries

ISBN: 978-1-7346669-5-3

DEDICATED TO:

Helen Barker-McClatchey
Jennie Barker-Ayers
Rev. Doug Barker
Bob Barker
Pam Barker-Reeves

We grew up together, laughed together, and loved the Lord together. You have been the best siblings a brother can have.

TABLE OF CONTENTS

The Christ

Revelation 1:1-20

The revelation of Jesus Christ, which God gave him to show to his servants the things that must soon take place. He made it known by sending his angel to his servant John, who bore witness to the word of God and to the testimony of Jesus Christ, even to all that he saw. Blessed is the one who reads aloud the words of this prophecy, and blessed are those who hear, and who keep what is written in it, for the time is near.

John to the seven churches that are in Asia: Grace to you and peace from him who is and who was and who is to come, and from the seven spirits who are before his throne, and from Jesus Christ the faithful witness, the firstborn of the dead, and the ruler of kings on earth. To him who loves us and has freed us from our sins by his blood and made us a kingdom, priests to his God and Father, to him be glory and dominion forever and ever. Amen. Behold, he is coming with the clouds, and every eye will see him, even those who pierced him, and all tribes of the earth will wail on account of him. Even so. Amen.

"I am the Alpha and the Omega," says the Lord God, "who is and who was and who is to come, the Almighty."

I, John, your brother and partner in the tribulation and the kingdom and the patient endurance that are in Jesus, was on the island called Patmos on account of the word of God and the testimony of Jesus. I was in the Spirit on the Lord's day, and I heard behind me a loud voice like a trumpet saying, "Write what you see in a book and send it to the seven churches, to Ephesus and to Smyrna and to Pergamum and to Thyatira and to Sardis and to Philadelphia and to Laodicea."

Then I turned to see the voice that was speaking to me, and on turning I saw seven golden lampstands, and in the midst of the lampstands one like a son of man, clothed with a long robe and with a golden sash around his chest. The hairs of his head were white, like white wool, like snow. His eyes were like a flame of fire, his feet were like burnished bronze, refined in a furnace, and his voice was like the roar

of many waters. In his right hand he held seven
stars, from his mouth came a sharp two-edged
sword, and his face was like the sun shining in full
strength.

When I saw him, I fell at his feet as though dead.
But he laid his right hand on me, saying, "Fear not,
I am the first and the last, and the living one. I died,
and behold I am alive forevermore, and I have the
keys of Death and Hades. Write therefore the
things that you have seen, those that are and those
that are to take place after this. As for the mystery
of the seven stars that you saw in my right hand,
and the seven golden lampstands, the seven stars
are the angels of the seven churches, and the seven
lampstands are the seven churches.

The book of Revelation is often ignored in Bible study groups, and even by preachers because of all the difficult symbolism and sometimes vague-sounding visions ... but it is the one book in the Bible that God promises a special blessing to those who simply read it (Rev. 1:3).

Another reason it is often ignored is because it is not understood correctly, and the focus of those who study it is skewed toward trying to piece together a detailed plan of the future. While there certainly are predictive elements to the book about the future, this is not the total focus of the book. Even its title should help us see this. It is NOT "THE REVELATION OF THE FUTURE" but "THE REVELATION OF JESUS CHRIST." It is as much about Christ as it is about the future! In fact, this is where the book begins ... one cannot look to the future without first coming to Christ who holds the future! Without Christ there is no guaranteed future, and without hope for a future there is no striving to be better!

The fact is that only Christians have a firm conviction that the future is certain, and we have this because of the book of Revelation which clearly says that God is in control ... we have a future to look forward to!

The book of Revelation shows us the glorified Christ and the certainty of His ruling over all things ... we are not stumbling toward an uncertain future ... but we will not enjoy this future if we are not in fellowship with the King!

There would be no reason to detail the future without first detailing who is in control of it ... and so the book of Revelation begins with a vision of Christ, not a vision of future details of history! John reveals Christ differently here from the Gospels. In the Gospels we are introduced to the baby Jesus, the Son of man, the one who was the suffering servant ... who willingly subjected Himself to wicked humanity and died for our sins. This was Jesus at His first coming ... a man that most were not afraid of, nor was Rome impressed with Him ... and certainly the Jews didn't take Him seriously for the most part.

Jesus in the Gospels is the man of sorrow, acquainted with grief, pierced with our iniquities, etc. But here John REVEALS Christ as the King of Glory! Jesus here is the conqueror, the one in charge of history, the one who alone controls the future, controls the nations, controls all the universe! This is the Jesus who is coming!

We must see this Jesus for faith in the future! No other leader has ever emerged that controls the future!

The tragic arrogance of man that keeps him from coming to God is that he believes he is in control of the future without God. This revelation that ONLY God controls the future should bring us to our knees to acknowledge Him as Lord! John's view of the future begins with Christ ... and so must ours!

John's vision of Revelation moves from Christ to the church ... the body of Christ! The church is not some passive actor on the stage of life. Jesus as King rules not only the universe, but His church as well.

One day the church will rule with Him all of creation!

This vision is given to John to awaken the church to both who Jesus Christ is as the risen Lord, the Lord of the second coming, and also to call the church to prepare for the future as the ruling body of Christ! We cannot afford to be lax in our living as His church; we should be planning on the future!

This revelation was to stir the church to be on guard, to live knowing that Christ's return is imminent, that God has a plan that we are to be ready for.

In fact, as we will discover, the first part of the book reveals the coming of King Jesus in power ... and the next part contains messages to the churches about being ready and impacting the world while there is still time.

This revelation is given to rouse the church to impact the world, to get its own house in order ... to be at the ready for Christ's triumphant return. The church cannot take the luxury of deciding it has plenty of time. There is a sense of immediacy and urgency to the book of Revelation. The early church expected Christ's return at any moment ... and so should we ... we are closer now to His return than at any other time in history!

John is clear in the Revelation given him that the church is called to be a nation of priests to serve God

... we are on a mission, a time-sensitive one!

John now turns to the future, but still with Christ as the focal point! He sees Jesus in power. The people of the earth when they view Christ will mourn ... those who don't know Him as Savior, that is. Jesus is shown now as the "Alpha and Omega" - the first and the last! Christ is over all things. This is more than the suffering servant; it is the ruling king!

Jesus will reveal to John a broad-stroke picture of the future. These rumblings of what is to come were meant to cause both the church and the world to get ready ... to prepare for the future God has planned.

As Michael Bogart of Lemoore, California, says in *Leadership*, Vol. 6, no. 4, just as a volcano rumbles its warning before erupting its destruction on the surrounding land, so our society is rumbling with the warning that Christ's return is near. With God, we have an escape provided for us.

Such warnings should not be ignored, yet too often they are! Today, many people ignore the teaching of the church that Jesus is coming back again ... this will prove very unfortunate for those who ignore the opportunity NOW. Even more tragic is that some churches don't preach or teach about the second of Christ anymore! How can this be!!!???

This REVELATION was being given to John to send

to the seven churches. The world will not prepare if the church does not! Knowledge about the future was not intended to satisfy our curiosity about specific details on tomorrow. It was meant to change us in the present as we realize that He is coming again with a certain future! It also was meant to show that evil will not triumph over God or His church. The seven churches were being asked to take seriously the future by living seriously in the present, with the implication that there are practical purposes to prophecy!

This REVELATION from God was meant to drive home the fact that death is the not the final end ... there are serious things to consider, because we continue to live after death!

The seven lampstands are the seven churches. Notice that Christ is said to be "among the lampstands" — He is among His church! Even in the frightening pictures of disaster that Revelation will later speak about, there should be calm in the church, for Christ is among the church! The second coming of Christ is our blessed hope!

Again, John sees the glorified Christ, brilliant and powerful ... this picture of Christ's supremacy was meant to inspire fear in the ungodly, but calm to the godly! Many times Jesus used the phrase with those

He loved, "Do not be afraid, it is I" (or "fear not"). This view of Jesus is one of power, absolute power ... nothing is greater than Christ and this alone should have allayed any fears or nervousness they might have had about the future. Jesus alone holds the keys of hell and death ... and for those who belong to Him, the future is only a good one!

Not only was Jesus among the seven lampstands, the church ... but it also says He held in His hand the seven stars ... the seven stars are said to the be "angels" of the seven churches ... meaning the "messengers" or pastors! (Greek word here "aggelos" [angelos] can mean either supernatural or natural messengers.) What a comfort to every pastor ... especially when they feel their work is in vain, to know that God holds every pastor who is preaching the truth in His hand! As John is about to reveal frightening details about the future, they are only frightening to those who have no relationship with God. For those who belong to Christ, these frightening events are simply assurances that tomorrow belongs to God and so do those who belong to Him, thus they calm us about the future!

We cannot miss the meaning of this book to reveal Christ in His power and glory and to reveal the future as under God's control.

To figure out the date of Jesus' second coming, or who the person will be who will become the Antichrist, is not the thrust of the book. The thrust of The Revelation of Jesus Christ is to reveal Jesus Christ and His control over tomorrow … and to be ready for the future when it gets here! And it will get here! And only those who belong to Christ will welcome it and benefit from it. Are you ready for the future?

The book of Revelation is first and foremost a revelation about Jesus, not just the future — even the title of the book suggests this: "THE REVELATION OF JESUS CHRIST." The focus is not just the future, it is the power of God in control of the future. You can get lost in the symbols and miss the message — the message is simply, "GOD HAS A PLAN FOR TOMOR-ROW — AND HIS CHURCH WILL BE TRIUMPHANT!"

What is your hope of the future based on, and are you ready for it?

The Churches

Revelation 2:1-3:22

"To the angel of the church in Ephesus write: 'The words of him who holds the seven stars in his right hand, who walks among the seven golden lampstands.

"'I know your works, your toil and your patient endurance, and how you cannot bear with those who are evil, but have tested those who call themselves apostles and are not, and found them to be false. I know you are enduring patiently and bearing up for my name's sake, and you have not grown weary. But I have this against you, that you have abandoned the love you had at first. Remember therefore from where you have fallen; repent, and do the works you did at first. If not, I will come to you and remove your lampstand from its place, unless you repent. Yet this you have: you

hate the works of the Nicolaitans, which I also hate. He who has an ear, let him hear what the Spirit says to the churches. To the one who conquers I will grant to eat of the tree of life, which is in the paradise of God.'

"And to the angel of the church in Smyrna write: 'The words of the first and the last, who died and came to life.

"'I know your tribulation and your poverty (but you are rich) and the slander of those who say that they are Jews and are not, but are a synagogue of Satan. Do not fear what you are about to suffer. Behold, the devil is about to throw some of you into prison, that you may be tested, and for ten days you will have tribulation. Be faithful unto death, and I will give you the crown of life. He who has an ear, let him hear what the Spirit says to the churches. The one who conquers will not be hurt by the second death.'

"And to the angel of the church in Pergamum write: 'The words of him who has the sharp two-edged sword.

"'I know where you dwell, where Satan's throne is. Yet you hold fast my name, and you did not deny my faith even in the days of Antipas my faithful witness, who was killed among you, where Satan dwells. But I have a few things against you: you

have some there who hold the teaching of Balaam, who taught Balak to put a stumbling block before the sons of Israel, so that they might eat food sacrificed to idols and practice sexual immorality. So also you have some who hold the teaching of the Nicolaitans. Therefore repent. If not, I will come to you soon and war against them with the sword of my mouth. He who has an ear, let him hear what the Spirit says to the churches. To the one who conquers I will give some of the hidden manna, and I will give him a white stone, with a new name written on the stone that no one knows except the one who receives it.'

"And to the angel of the church in Thyatira write: 'The words of the Son of God, who has eyes like a flame of fire, and whose feet are like burnished bronze.

"'I know your works, your love and faith and service and patient endurance, and that your latter works exceed the first. But I have this against you, that you tolerate that woman Jezebel, who calls herself a prophetess and is teaching and seducing my servants to practice sexual immorality and to eat food sacrificed to idols. I gave her time to repent, but she refuses to repent of her sexual immorality. Behold, I will throw her onto a sickbed, and those who commit adultery with her I will

throw into great tribulation, unless they repent of
her works, and I will strike her children dead. And
all the churches will know that I am he who
searches mind and heart, and I will give to each of
you according to your works. But to the rest of you
in Thyatira, who do not hold this teaching, who
have not learned what some call the deep things of
Satan, to you I say, I do not lay on you any other
burden. Only hold fast what you have until I come.
The one who conquers and who keeps my works
until the end, to him I will give authority over the
nations, and he will rule them with a rod of iron, as
when earthen pots are broken in pieces, even as I
myself have received authority from my Father.
And I will give him the morning star. He who has an
ear, let him hear what the Spirit says to the
churches.'

"And to the angel of the church in Sardis write:
'The words of him who has the seven spirits of God
and the seven stars.

"'I know your works. You have the reputation of
being alive, but you are dead. Wake up, and
strengthen what remains and is about to die, for I
have not found your works complete in the sight of
my God. Remember, then, what you received and
heard. Keep it, and repent. If you will not wake up,
I will come like a thief, and you will not know at

what hour I will come against you. Yet you have still a few names in Sardis, people who have not soiled their garments, and they will walk with me in white, for they are worthy. The one who conquers will be clothed thus in white garments, and I will never blot his name out of the book of life. I will confess his name before my Father and before his angels. He who has an ear, let him hear what the Spirit says to the churches.'

"And to the angel of the church in Philadelphia write: 'The words of the holy one, the true one, who has the key of David, who opens and no one will shut, who shuts and no one opens.

"'I know your works. Behold, I have set before you an open door, which no one is able to shut. I know that you have but little power, and yet you have kept my word and have not denied my name. Behold, I will make those of the synagogue of Satan who say that they are Jews and are not, but lie—behold, I will make them come and bow down before your feet, and they will learn that I have loved you. Because you have kept my word about patient endurance, I will keep you from the hour of trial that is coming on the whole world, to try those who dwell on the earth. I am coming soon. Hold fast what you have, so that no one may seize your crown. The one who conquers, I will make him a

25

pillar in the temple of my God. Never shall he go out of it, and I will write on him the name of my God, and the name of the city of my God, the new Jerusalem, which comes down from my God out of heaven, and my own new name. He who has an ear, let him hear what the Spirit says to the churches.'

"And to the angel of the church in Laodicea write: 'The words of the Amen, the faithful and true witness, the beginning of God's creation.

"'I know your works: you are neither cold nor hot. Would that you were either cold or hot! So, because you are lukewarm, and neither hot nor cold, I will spit you out of my mouth. For you say, I am rich, I have prospered, and I need nothing, not realizing that you are wretched, pitiable, poor, blind, and naked. I counsel you to buy from me gold refined by fire, so that you may be rich, and white garments so that you may clothe yourself and the shame of your nakedness may not be seen, and salve to anoint your eyes, so that you may see. Those whom I love, I reprove and discipline, so be zealous and repent. Behold, I stand at the door and knock. If anyone hears my voice and opens the door, I will come in to him and eat with him, and he with me. The one who conquers, I will grant him to sit with me on my throne, as I also conquered and

sat down with my Father on his throne. He who has an ear, let him hear what the Spirit says to the churches.'"

Revelation starts off with a vision of Christ. We cannot see the future if we don't first see Christ clearly. Next it stops at the churches before moving to the future. The church cannot hope for a future if it doesn't live right in the present!

There is yet no unfolding of the future in the book, no revelation of tomorrow until the churches have a clear understanding of what it means to be the church TODAY! These seven churches which represent all churches everywhere needed some guidance about how they lived NOW before being given promises of what tomorrow would hold. How often we love prophecies about the future and avoid the need of living for God in the present … this won't do in the book of Revelation. God addresses the needs of the church now before moving on to tomorrow … so should we!

If I put in the paper for the upcoming Sunday an announcement that I would unveil what the future holds, there would not be one empty seat in the church! But promising to address the needs of the church today would hardly make a difference in the attendance!

The Scriptures teach us that the secret to tomorrow is wrapped up in how we live today! The key to the future is what we do today ... we cannot ignore the present for prophecy!

Each of the seven churches is addressed similarly: "I know ..." God is very much aware of each church's situation and health. We may wonder sometimes if God cares about us or our church but be assured that He does! Nothing escapes His notice, concern, or praise.

These seven churches each were unique, and each had strengths and weaknesses. Each needed direction from God. God always has something to say to His church. God is anxious for His church to be all that it can be.

Each church and each believer had to face both good and bad times. It would be how they handled both that would determine their future ... and often wealth and success were more dangerous than failure and poverty!

Their individual situations were quite diverse, but their responsibilities were the same. No matter in good or bad times, they were to remain faithful to God. Ironically, it was the few churches in poverty that had the best things said about them, and the wealthiest of the seven churches that had the harshest things said about them.

God was not nearly as concerned about the churches' material wealth as He was about their spiritual wealth! God has some important things to share with each of these churches and the believers that were a part of them, messages we still need to hear!

EPHESUS — This was a second-generation church. Its founders had been hard-working, had established a thriving, growing church ... but now a new generation had grown up in the church that did not have the same passion as their pioneers! Ephesus was the city of LOVE! One of the seven wonders of the ancient world was in this city, the temple of LOVE to Artemis or Diana. Ironically, the very name "EPHESUS" means "Desirable" — yet the desire to serve the Lord in this church had waned! In the CITY OF LOVE, the church had lost its FIRST LOVE! The city was steeped in LUST while the church didn't even have LOVE anymore! They needed to do three things:

1. "Remember the height from which you have fallen."

2. "Repent."

3. "Redo the things you did at first."

Restoration was the idea here, restoration to the same first passion that caused their testimony to exist in the first place! It is too easy for any church to lose its passion for Christ and ministry … God help us that it doesn't happen here!

SMYRNA — This was one of the poorest of the seven churches. It was a large city, and trade guilds were important, but to be a part of one you had to worship idols in the pagan temples. Because Christians would not compromise their standards, they were kicked out of the trade guilds and were left largely to poverty. BUT Jesus says that He knows their "poverty, that they are rich." Nothing negative about this church … only praise and encouragement not to give in, even to the point of death … and a real crown awaits them! This would have been the church to complain, but they passionately lived for Christ despite the cost personally to them … can you say the same? Christ promises them that they "would suffer for 10 days," simply meaning that God would limit the time of their suffering. He is in control.

PERGAMUM — This was the Washington D.C. of Asia at the time. It was a political capital, and a large healing cult existed there. Worship of Asclepius, the healing god, was big, symbolized by a serpent wound around a staff (still the symbol of the healing profession in our country today!!). There was a huge library with over 200,000 volumes! A huge altar over 40 feet high was in this city. Today it has been moved to Berlin, Germany, after being excavated! Emperor worship was common here, and the pressures to compromise with the world were strong. The governor of Asia resided in this city, and he had a sword which symbolized his power of IUS GLADII, which meant the "right of the sword." He had the power to execute anyone at his will! Jesus however says He has a DOUBLE-EDGED SWORD — better and more powerful than the governor's! This was tantamount to saying, "My authority is greater!" and thus the church should not be afraid! The church was doing well for the most part, but a few people were promoting the teachings of Balaam, the prophet in the Old Testament that encouraged Israel to compromise their commitment to God by breaking God's laws. The seeds of compromise with the world were beginning to take root in this church. They needed to remember whose "sword" was greater, the governor's or God's!

THYATIRA — This was a blue-collar town, a very small town! Ironically, the smallest of the seven cities has the biggest message! God's value of a place is not determined by its size! Textiles and small trade guilds were important in this town. Unlike Ephesus, which had good doctrine and teaching but lacked passion, this blue-collar church had lots of passion but too little doctrine and teaching! They were too easily led astray. In fact, their passions had driven them to live undisciplined lives, so much so that sexual immorality was too often the result of unbridled passions, hence the comments in the passage about this. This was a church that needed discipline for its desires. We live in a culture of passions that often ignores discipline — the church cannot afford this mistake!

SARDIS — This was a horribly ungodly and immoral city. It boasted of its worship of Cybele, a mother goddess that included some very debased and perverted worship practices of a sexual nature. The city was on top of a steep hill, and so the city felt secure thinking no one could capture them ... the steep rocky hills would keep the enemy away! Because of this they often failed to post guards and were several times overrun by the enemy! Thieves often hid in the rocky cliffs and invaded the town. This fact sets the stage for God's comment to this church that if they didn't get their act together, "He would come as a thief!" This church was not almost dead, IT WAS DEAD! This was the worst of the seven churches ... its reputation was that it was alive, but they had already died! God calls them to "WAKE UP" (Rev. 3:2). Their false sense of security left them open to destruction, much like the city they lived in! A church can have God in its name, but not in its midst! God has almost nothing good to say about this church, and they are warned to turn around quickly before they are lost. You could only worship at the local temple if you had clean clothes on, so God says to them, "Yet, you have a few people in Sardis who have not soiled their clothes; they will walk with me dressed in white ..."

PHILADELPHIA — The city of earthquakes! So many that there were ruins everywhere where only the pillars of buildings were still standing! Notice that Jesus promises this church that those who overcome He will make a pillar in His temple! God promises "standing in the midst of shaking" to those who stay true to Him. This church has nothing bad said about it, because they were unshaken in a city that often was! This was a small church ... the meaning of the phrase "little strength" in the text. Their size, however, meant nothing, for they were giants in the faith! God promises this church that they will be kept from the trial that is going to come upon the whole world ... perhaps the tribulation period, although the term translated "FROM" can also be "THROUGH," so it cannot be certain here what is meant except that God will supernaturally protect them from some great trial to face the world.

LAODICEA — One of the largest and wealthiest cities ... so wealthy that when it was destroyed completely by an earthquake in 60 A.D. (about 30 years before Revelation was written) it rebuilt itself without any financial help from outsiders!! This was the self-reliant wealthy church. It was lukewarm! The city had hot water coming from Hierapolis six miles away through a huge aqueduct, and cold water from six miles in the other direction from the mountains nearby, ducted into the city because it had no natural water sources locally. HOWEVER, by the time the hot water and cold water reached the city, they were both lukewarm! It was not uncommon for local visitors going to one of the many fountains in the center of town expecting a cold drink of cool mountain water to gag on the lukewarm water and spit it out disappointed ... Jesus picks up on this image to tell this church how He feels with their lukewarmness! (Note: the word "SPIT" here literally is "VOMIT" in Greek.) Laodicea was also famous for an eye salve called Phrygian powder, world famous for its eye healing properties ... yet God says this church was "BLIND" and that they needed to buy from Him eye salve!

Jesus also says they are naked. The city was famous for its black cloth industry … but they needed white clothing from Him! Though wealthy, they were poor and needed to buy from Christ true gold refined in fire! There was a way out. They must get hot again!

Each church had been given a specific challenge, often related to things their city was famous for … what would God challenge us about? It was too easy for these second-generation churches to lose their fervency. What about us? Too often we are passionate about the wrong things!

How could God tell His church about the future until they had mastered the present? The first challenge isn't the future, it's the present! Can we identify what our challenges are today?

What about our temperature? Are we lukewarm? Do we have too little passion, too much, are we perhaps self-reliant and self-righteous? Do we compromise with the world's standards, or have we become a second-generation church with less commitment than the first? What specific challenge is God making of us in our present as we anticipate and wait for the future?

Each message ends similarly: "To him who overcomes … I will …" God makes promises to the overcomers, promises of power, of good! There is also a similar challenge: "He who has an ear, let him hear what the Spirit says to the churches." Are we listening? God does not ask us to respond without also promising supernatural help. That is the good news! Each of the churches had a supernatural commitment from God for help. They only had to have their present condition ready for tomorrow's action! Jesus IS coming again ... that's the future, but it is a future that depends on the present condition of our lives ... are you ready for His coming again? He will not leave us to our own resources. He has promised His own strength and help ... have you turned to Him for it? It is never too late to keep pressing on. There is more growing to do no matter how old we get!

W. Frank Harrington in *Preaching Today* tells of 90-year-old Pablo Casals who continues to practice his cello for hours each day. His reason? He says he feels younger and is confident that he improves musically after each session.

God knew each pastor and each church — their strengths and weaknesses. The strengths He praised and encouraged them to continue, while their weaknesses were addressed and challenged for change. IF they changed and accepted the challenge, God promised power, placement, and privilege; punishment was reserved only for the hardest of hearts. God will keep those who try — they will triumphantly reign with Christ.

Do you have ears and eyes to hear and see?

Love Lost!

Revelation 2:1-7

"To the angel of the church in Ephesus write: 'The words of him who holds the seven stars in his right hand, who walks among the seven golden lampstands.

"'I know your works, your toil and your patient endurance, and how you cannot bear with those who are evil, but have tested those who call themselves apostles and are not, and found them to be false. I know you are enduring patiently and bearing up for my name's sake, and you have not grown weary. But I have this against you, that you have abandoned the love you had at first. Remember therefore from where you have fallen; repent, and do the works you did at first. If not, I will come to you and remove your lampstand from its place, unless you repent. Yet this you have: you

hate the works of the Nicolaitans, which I also hate. He who has an ear, let him hear what the Spirit says to the churches. To the one who conquers I will grant to eat of the tree of life, which is in the paradise of God.'"

SALT! We use it to spice up our food, to add flavor to it, to preserve, to help in healing, to cleanse, etc. Salt is a necessity in our diet; we would die without it! In antiquity it was considered so important that at times it was more valuable than gold and was used sometimes as hard currency! Salt is made up of only two elements: SODIUM & CHLORINE (thus: Sodium Chloride). Like Christianity ... made up of two elements: TRUTH & LOVE. Combined, they are wonderful ... but either existing alone brings death!

Truth without love is like chlorine ... chlorine without sodium is a poisonous gas; it is what gives bleach its distinctive offensive odor. Chlorine is used to purify, but alone it is a killer! Love is like sodium ... sodium is almost never found in nature without combining itself to some other element. It is an extremely active agent. If chlorine isn't available, it will combine with something else. Love is like this. IT IS NOT ENOUGH to JUST love, for without truth, love combines with all kinds of things and can produce strange substances!

THE CHURCH MUST COMBINE BOTH TRUTH & LOVE ... like salt ... in order to be useful!

The church in Ephesus was missing LOVE. Though they maintained truth, they had lost an important element. The passion of their faith and service was missing. Yes, it can happen!

The Bible teaches us that if we lose our "first love" for Christ, our service will become weary, and the results will be just another institution attempting to create another product! God calls us to have passion in our service for Him, and when we do, our ministry becomes a JOY rather than just a JOB!

It is hard not to like this church at Ephesus! It was a church of workers! These were not lazy Christians ... God even states this clearly! How many churches today would pass this same test!? These were not sporadic Christians ... they were hard workers all the time! This was their earned reputation!

The city of Ephesus was a unique city, with a population of 250,000 people!!! It was the chief seaport of Asia ... nearly all goods from east to west went through Ephesus. The theater in Ephesus seated 25,000 people at one time! Its roads were wide, its homes spacious, its buildings elaborate. It was a tourist town! It was also very religious ... having dozens of temples to various gods and goddesses. One of the seven wonders of the world was in Ephesus ... the temple to ARTEMIS (also called Diana). The temple was 425 feet long, adorned with gold, marble, and all kinds of jewels, and maintained about 1,000 prostitutes in the temple ... ARTEMIS was the "goddess of LOVE!" Even the city's name reflects this: "EPHESUS" means "Desirable" or "Maiden of Choice."

The church was probably the largest church in its day! This church had entered its second generation! It was established by Paul around 50-60 A.D. It was a well-established church, with a reputation of high degree ... but the church was at a spiritual crossroads as far as God was concerned. How ironic that its problem was that of LOVE in the very town where the "love goddess" was strongest! There was nothing wrong with their service and works, but they were losing their passion for God. In a town that held a premium on passion, this could easily become a liability and snag to the Gospel!

Why was this so critical? If their ministry was duty alone, the people of the town would fail to see a difference between REAL LOVE and that of LUST! In other words, the church might lose its relevancy! They would even be LESS of a draw than the passionate worship of ARTEMIS! It would have been like trying to attract a football fanatic who jumps and gets into the game to a baseball game ... with a stadium full of spectators that did nothing but sit there and write statistics on the game and show no emotions! They had the perfect opportunity to show the Ephesians the difference between passion for the right God and passion that turned to lust for a false god, but to do this they would have to recapture their lost love for God! God wasn't asking them for more work ... just motivation based on loving God as they once had!

They not only worked hard, they were not quitters! They persevered! They kept up their ministry no matter the odds against them! They were not easily sidetracked by opposition. They were stalwarts of good doctrine and teaching. They even knew how to spot false teachers. They did not become weary in the battle!

God commends them for this stability. Being a second-generation church had given adequate time to really develop their teaching and programs, and yet, something quite important was still missing, something important enough to endanger their lampstand from continuing!!! What was missing by this church was its PASSION OR LOVE!

They were not far from being like the Temple of

Artemis!! HOW, YOU ASK? At the Temple of Artemis, there was all kinds of activity ... but no REAL LOVE (just lust!). If they as a church had lost their love, then they would be left with all kinds of activity but no real love! When that happens, the world only sees the church as nothing more than just another social institution! (HOW PROPHETIC OF MANY CHURCHES TODAY!) They could have all the outward appearances of worship and service and still be empty ... sooner or later it would show! How sad for a Christian or a church to settle for just ritual ... forsaken of passion! Passion can sometimes do more than programs!

The church in Ephesus was in danger of being without the passion needed in their service of God and therefore without attraction to the citizens of Ephesus! This would be a reckless mistake ... why reckless? Because it didn't have to be! There was no cost involved ... no resources not already available! To ignore this need would be a reckless error in a town of people whose means of support and recreation were founded on a goddess of love! Their lampstand (the church) existed in this town so that these people could know the difference between LUST and LOVE! For them to ignore LOVE would leave the people without a way to know the difference!

This is true today of the church: IF WE DON'T LOVE

GOD AND ONE ANOTHER our society will degenerate into a society based on LUST ... never knowing the difference between the two! What if we fail to really love God properly? What if we fail to really love one another properly? What model will the world have if we don't become that model!!!?

A loveless church or Christian is a serious offense to God! A bickering, backbiting church has little appeal for the Gospel of Jesus Christ! A church that only loves truth and not each other is in danger of losing their lampstand ... and light! This would indeed be a reckless thing in God's kingdom!

God doesn't leave them with the problem ... He offers a solution. THANK GOD! The starting point of repairing the problem was in remembering the past! Those who forget the good things of God in the past will lose their passion for God in the future! (It happened all the time to Israel when one generation failed to remember what God had done for their forefathers!) They were to remember the days of passion! All they had to do was remember that past passion to ignite their passions of self-sacrifice!

Sometimes it is good for us to remember the passion in which we served God after we first got saved ... a fresh dose can come from a fresh memory!

Now comes a surprise correction item:

REPENTANCE! This word is hardly spoken in the church anymore. Nobody thinks they need it, or it is just too old-fashioned ... not cultured! But after remembering, God hoped those memories would jolt them to action. Repentance was TURNING AROUND 180 degrees from where they were going!

Repentance has never been a popular thing to preach ... or practice! BUT IT IS A POWERFUL WITNESS FOR THE POWER OF THE GOSPEL! Noah's message from the ark was not, "SOMETHING GOOD IS GOING TO HAPPEN TO YOU!" Amos was not confronted by the High Priest of Israel for proclaiming, "CONFESSION IS POSSESSION!" Jeremiah was not put into the pit for preaching, "POSSIBILITY THINKING WILL MOVE MOUNTAINS!" Daniel was not put into the lion's den for telling people, "I'M O.K., YOU'RE O.K.!" John the Baptist was not forced to preach in the wilderness and eventually beheaded because he preached, "SMILE, GOD LOVES YOU!" THEY ALL preached repentance! Turn around before it's too late! SIMPLE, but PRO-FOUND!

The church was called not only to remember, but to repent ... do something different, go back to their first love. SOMETIMES THE ROAD TO PROGRESS IS FOUND IN REVERSE!!!!! For this church to move forward it had to turn around!

The final remedial item is REPETITION! It seems strange, but they are being called to re-run their previous record but with the passion they had lost! It doesn't take some new thrilling program to revitalize a church ... but it does take a repeating of the passion that once built that church! Some of the best things in life have been around a long time, and they are worth repeating!

Over and over again the prophets spoke the same message ... Israel, though, wanted to hear something NEW AND DIFFERENT! This will characterize the last days before Christ's triumphant return, people wanting new teaching! Master the old stuff first ... there is nothing new under the sun, anyway!

During this renewal of passion, God states the importance of keeping that passion focused properly, hating the practices of sin and NOT the sinners! Perhaps God added this knowing the dangers of passion rekindled could also create a passion that moves in the wrong direction. This was added to guard against their new-found passion corrupting the opportunities! Hate the right THINGS! Don't hate PEOPLE!

As a challenge to properly see the difference, God added the next line: "He who has ears to hear, let him hear!"

TAKE NOTE ... and HEAR CORRECTLY! This is not something from the mind of man; this comes from the Spirit of God! We need a discerning heart these days to separate hatred towards the right targets and to see the need of our own heart!

A promise is held out for those who hear and respond correctly: "THE TREE OF LIFE!" A new homeland awaits those who not only serve but serve with a real passion for God! The result of serving with passion is GREAT PASSION ... PARADISE WITH GOD! A great joy awaits those who serve with it!

THE WARNING SIGNS OF LOST PASSION IN SERVICE:

- apathy about service
- joyless experience ... the "I'll do it if I have to"
- bitter spirit
- judgmental heart toward others
- boredom
- pride rather than passion
- frequent complaining

It is possible for both the believer and the church to be active in God's work and yet be dead spiritually! Life without love is not righteousness, just ritual! JOY is replaced by JOB when God's love is absent in our hearts. Over time, passion can be lost to programs ...

we need to renew our first love for God if we hope to escape empty rituals!

Rich Poverty!

Revelation 2:8-11; James 1:2-4, 12

"And to the angel of the church in Smyrna write: 'The words of the first and the last, who died and came to life.

"'I know your tribulation and your poverty (but you are rich) and the slander of those who say that they are Jews and are not, but are a synagogue of Satan. Do not fear what you are about to suffer. Behold, the devil is about to throw some of you into prison, that you may be tested, and for ten days you will have tribulation. Be faithful unto death, and I will give you the crown of life. He who has an ear, let him hear what the Spirit says to the churches. The one who conquers will not be hurt by the second death.'"

Count it all joy, my brothers, when you meet trials

of various kinds, for you know that the testing of your faith produces steadfastness. And let steadfastness have its full effect, that you may be perfect and complete, lacking in nothing.

Blessed is the man who remains steadfast under trial, for when he has stood the test he will receive the crown of life, which God has promised to those who love him.

In Western society we have been raised to believe that wealth brings happiness and joy ... that poverty brings pain and ignorance. Our lives are heavily geared around making more money, gaining more things, always looking for carefree living.

Ironically, those who are the wealthiest are far from the happiest people. The Bible teaches that there are two kinds of wealth ... that of this world, and that of the kingdom of God!

While the world's wealth is not easy to gain, that of the kingdom is available to all at any time! Many times worldly wealth gets in the way of spiritual wealth, hence Jesus' statement to His disciples that "it is easier for a camel to go through the eye of a needle than for a rich man to enter the kingdom of God!"

Do we seek spiritual riches with the same tenacity

and efforts that we seek worldly wealth? The Bible teaches that true wealth often comes when we are without this world's wealth. Some of God's great principles of life are best learned in the absence of worldly goods. Suffering is a better teacher than prosperity! Like the crushing of flowers … it is in the crushing that the fragrance is released to bless others nearby!

The city of Smyrna, unlike some of the other six churches mentioned here, is today still one of the largest cities in that area (the city of Izmir in Turkey). The church here has no word of condemnation by God … they were a godly church! The city had a large group of Jewish citizens that were very hostile to the Christians. It was one of the few cities of the time to have a temple for emperor worship.

The name of this city, Smyrna, literally means "bitter" or "myrrh." Myrrh was a perfume used for burials. It was made from a tree resin that was beaten to bring out its fragrance.

The city was known as the city "WHO DIED AND CAME TO LIFE AGAIN." It had been destroyed at one point … and much later resurrected back to life! Jesus mentions it in Revelation 2:8: "To the angel of the church in Smyrna write: These are the words of him who is the First and the Last, who died and came to life again." The citizens used this expression to brag about its newfound life! Remember the introduction of Jesus to this church!!

The city was also famous for its games ... and garland wreathes for winners!

The city had powerful trade guilds. Major industries included idolatry, such as the great temple to Bacchus, the god of wine. The poverty of these Christians was undoubtedly related to these trade guilds. These uncompromising Christians were kicked out of the trade guilds, thus losing their means of living. They gradually entered into poverty, abject poverty! Many of them who once had thriving businesses were forced into bankruptcy or compromise ... and they chose bankruptcy over compromise! Those who had been part of the Jewish community were now declared "non-Jews." They were no longer considered by the Jewish community a part of "God's chosen people!" They lost their cultural identity because of their commitment to Christ. They lost their means of living. They lost their wealth. They lost their acceptance by others outside the church.

They were experiencing bitter suffering and loss without reason of sin in their lives and struggling with the issue of why a loving and good God would allow this in light of their obvious faithfulness to Christ!

Though under stress, there is no hint whatsoever that they were complaining or bitter! In fact, the evidence in this text suggests the opposite!!

Sadly, there was no light at the end of the tunnel … God adds that more persecution lay ahead of them! The stress level would increase … and the persecution was now moving toward even death for those Christians.

As God's people, it is very clear that we are not immune from suffering, but we can avoid its NATURAL consequences such as anger and bitterness! The pressing circumstances had sharpened their perspective of what really matters in life. The pressures stripped them of focusing only on material things. Stripping away these other things had allowed them the freedom to center their attention on spiritual things.

The secret to surviving this kind of stress is proper focus! They had to see beyond the present troubles … to know that God doesn't allow suffering without purpose! Failure to focus right leads to despair! God's Word to them was this need for focus.

Our Christian life can be pictured as a cake mix. All the ingredients mixed create a wonderful delight to the palate; however, many of the ingredients alone would cause us to gag! Things like alum, baking powder, even flour alone would not excite us or taste good! It is all these things mixed in right amounts that make a wonderful cake! This is the meaning in Romans 8:28: "All things MIXED together work to our good!" — even the bitter stuff!

It is in this same context of a cake mix that we understand JAMES 1:2-4. We can be grateful for trials because of the fruit of what can come from the experience. We can know that it is these experiences that focus us on God and the spiritual realities that lead us to maturity! This maturity enables us to be strong in the Lord and the power of His might!

The secret to surviving spiritual suffering and loss is the knowledge of more than just the moment ... it is the knowledge that God works all things for our good. God will make a purpose for the suffering. Sometimes that purpose is to benefit others, or it may be to benefit us ... or it may just bring glory to God or encourage someone else who suffers! BUT it is never without some purpose. God's plan is good for us!

The church at Smyrna would be stronger spiritually because of what they went through and so would their testimony! Indeed, this proved to be true, even up to today! Because of their commitment to Christ, even today there is a thriving community of Christians within this same city, one of the largest cities in Turkey today! The very pastor who was killed from this church (John's disciple Polycarp) still has his grave within this modern city as a testimony of his faith! Their strength has given strength to others throughout the generations to hold fast to Christ!

The church's pastor at the time John wrote this was a man by the name of Polycarp. We know that he died in 155 A.D., and that his final statement before being burned at the stake was: "80 & 6 years I have served Him, and He never did me wrong; and how can I now blaspheme my King that has saved me!" He may well have pastored this church in Smyrna for almost 60 years, starting shortly after the book of Revelation was written. Thus, this prophecy may have been a source of strength for him and the church to be faithful! Ironically ... those Jews who burned him at the stake did so on a Sabbath, gathering the wood against their own laws!

Trials are never intended by God to destroy us, but to make us stronger! Strength is created and shown by trials, not in the absence of them!

The great surprise is that though poor by this world's standards we are becoming rich by God's standards! It is also important to note that God says, "You will suffer ... for 10 days ..." God would limit the duration of that suffering. It would not go on forever!

Thus, He is in control of all things, even pain! Their loss was very real and very painful. The word used for "poverty" in the earlier verse (v. 9) was the Greek word for "ABJECT POVERTY"... not just "poor." Also, the word used for "afflictions" (v. 9) translates literally as "SERIOUS TROUBLE" or "A BURDEN THAT CRUSHES" — not just inconvenience! But it would all lead to a great payment of wealth for them! Their poverty was driving them toward wealth in God! While painful for the moment, they were becoming a masterpiece of craftsmanship to adorn God's holy temple! The great surprise is that they were not getting poorer but richer! If they were faithful, even to death, they still would be ahead ... for their faithfulness they were promised the "crown of life." This meant eternal life ... billions of years of existence with all of God's wealth for the faithfulness of a few dozen years on earth! The exchange rate is unbelievable!

In the end, the balances will reverse. Those who were wealthy on earth but ignored God would die and leave it all behind; in death they will be completely barren ... full poverty! But for these Christians who in life had nothing, in death they would have everything!

Those with spiritual hearing will understand the role of suffering and the rewards of it! They will be secure even when life now robs them of all securities! They will recognize the end product ... security in God!

They also understand that death will not hurt them or leave them stripped ... but in fact will usher them into great wealth and life that can never be taken from them! They live in the present pain with the knowledge of the future for their peace and prosperity! This is what provided them their security ... eternal life in Christ! Though they were poor ... they really were quite rich!

It is the wind and rain as they roll across the earth that break the elements found in nature into rich soil, out of which comes the vital growth of plants that supply the fruits that sustain us! So it is with storms of life ... they break down our arrogance and independence, causing us to depend on God and producing in us the fruits of righteousness. An occasional storm can enhance spiritual realities ... grow rich in your poverty!

Sword vs. the Serpent!

Revelation 2:12-17

"And to the angel of the church in Pergamum write: 'The words of him who has the sharp two-edged sword.

"'I know where you dwell, where Satan's throne is. Yet you hold fast my name, and you did not deny my faith even in the days of Antipas my faithful witness, who was killed among you, where Satan dwells. But I have a few things against you: you have some there who hold the teaching of Balaam, who taught Balak to put a stumbling block before the sons of Israel, so that they might eat food sacrificed to idols and practice sexual immorality. So also you have some who hold the teaching of the Nicolaitans. Therefore repent. If not, I will come to you soon and war against them with the sword of my mouth. He who has an ear, let him hear

*what the Spirit says to the churches. To the one
who conquers I will give some of the hidden
manna, and I will give him a white stone, with a
new name written on the stone that no one knows
except the one who receives it.'"*

The Human body is remarkably adaptable. One unique feature is our body's ability to tolerate pain. You can teach yourself to tolerate greater and greater degrees of pain by slow doses of increased amounts of pain. Unfortunately, pain medications do the same thing in our body. Pain relieving medications can be a wonderful help ... but if they are taken too frequently and close together, our body becomes tolerant of the drug and the doses must be increased in strength and frequency to continue helping. The frequent exposure can dull our response until it is withdrawn, then oh, the pain! Sin can be like this. Constant or frequent exposure to it can make us less sensitive to its true nature until we are very comfortable tolerating sin in our own life. We may even be unaware of sin until the Holy Spirit withdraws ... then oh, the pain!

One of the true great dangers to the church and the believer is that of tolerance of sin in our own life and a compromising heart with this world! A church can survive many vicious attacks, but a slow gradual slide toward the world can go unnoticed. We are asked to have one heart for God. To scoop our joys from the world and mix that with God's provisions is to compromise the witness of the uniqueness of the kingdom, to pollute ourselves. The Bible teaches us that we are to carefully guard our hearts from this world's pollution! Trying to mix Christianity with worldliness will only contaminate the Gospel of grace! Tolerating sin in our life will surely lead to spiritual ineffectiveness!

The City of Pergamum today exists as Bergama, Turkey. Its name means "Citadel" (fortress or place of safety). While Ephesus and Smyrna reigned as commercial capitals, Pergamum was the Washington D.C. of Asia of the time. It was the political capital. It also was well known for its medical & educational prowess, with a large and very prominent temple to the god Askelpios — the cult god of healing (symbolized by a serpent around a staff … the same symbol still used today for doctors!). People with all kinds of ailments flocked to the temple grounds and waited for the priests to mingle through the crowds with magical cures. A large library containing parchment books was in Pergamum — in fact, the word "parchment" comes from the root name of this city. The library was large and extensive: 200,000 volumes! Anthony sent this entire library to Egypt as a gift to Cleopatra! A huge altar (40 feet) was on the top of a hill. Today this altar has been excavated and now resides in East Berlin, Germany!

The governor of Asia resided here. He was the official "champion of justice"... and also the leader of emperor worship. He had as a symbol a sword, claiming in Latin "IUS GLADII"... the "right of the sword"... the power to execute anyone he willed! His authority by the symbol of this sword gave him absolute authority! Emperor worship was nothing more than the worship of man himself!

The pressures to compromise as a Christian were enormous!! For a Christian to live in this political city where the compromise of ethics was common was tough! The "everybody does it to get by" mentality was common! "That's just the way it is" was strong. "If you're honest they'll take you to the cleaners" mentality was invading the church!

It was getting hard to be a real Christian! No matter where in town you went, you were rubbing shoulders with immorality! To their credit, they are commended by the Lord for thus far holding firm ... but the seeds of decay were already in the church, the pressure of compromise!

In comparison to the governor's sword (IUS GLADII), Jesus' sword is two-edged! The sword of our Lord is a better sword ... thus a greater authority than the governor's! Two-edged meant it cut in both directions, with an edge to cut away the unwanted stuff and an edge to destroy enemies! (or perhaps the analogy of two edges meant to heal or hurt!)

The two-edged sword was the largest ... and longest ... and the most feared of offensive weapons in the sword family! Jesus was making a clear statement to a people who knew about the authority of the sword: "MY AUTHORITY IS GREATEST!"

"Where Satan has his throne" is probably a reference to emperor worship, or the worship of man (Humanism)! Also, it is likely a reference to the corrupt political system of immorality and poor ethics! It may have also included the many cults such as the healing cult of ASKLEPIOS that was prominent in the city ... Zeus' huge altar, etc. The city was steeped in immorality ... although it was very prosperous and the political capital of Asia!

We must recognize that evil has its grip on the world systems ... where God is mocked, Satan rules! This was an acknowledgement of REAL evil! To this church's credit ... they had done well so far in keeping a clear moral path, and they were commended for their faith thus far! They had not compromised yet, but the seeds were there in the church that would soon allow this to happen. They had remained faithful so far, even when one of their own was put to death. His name was ANTIPAS. His name means "AGAINST ALL"! This church member had been a man unwilling to compromise and his witness had guided them to keep a straight path.

With Antipas gone, however, other elements in the church were arising with the teachings of compromise. These "enlightened" members were encouraging acceptance of ungodly standards to avoid clashes with the community, probably under the guise of not wanting to offend the citizens they were trying to reach! The trouble with this mentality is that it just doesn't work. If we are JUST like the world, then there is no reason for the world to change! The trouble with "fighting fire with fire" is that even more stuff gets burned up! We can't win the lost by using unethical and immoral standards! And we can't make the Gospel more attractive by being like the world!

God had some concerns about this church and where they were heading! To point out this concern now before they lost their testimony was giving them the chance to do something early, before damage occurred! God loves us enough to challenge us ... even early!

The issue God had with the church was their willingness to hold to the teachings of Balaam! This reference was to the Old Testament "prophet" who was hired by the wicked King Balak of Moab to curse Israel. The curse did not work, so this so-called "prophet" shared with the Moabite king how Israel could be corrupted and thus have God Himself judge them. This would be almost as good as cursing them! The plan was to send Moabite women down to the camp of Israel and flirt with the Israeli men, thus getting them to partake of unkosher food and also commit immorality with them. Once they had flirted with these Moabite women, God would come down on them in judgment. Balaam knew God wouldn't curse them, but this judgment would take them out of commission for a while and allow the Moabites to continue — IT WORKED, sadly to say!

The issue was simple: God's concern for this church included some within the congregation that wanted to get rid of the teaching about sin! These people wanted to be accepted by the world more than by God. They didn't want to be thought of as "DIFFERENT." They were beginning to encourage more toleration and less teaching about sin — to be open minded! These would be the seeds of decline for spirituality within this church if this teaching was practiced! It is dangerous to compromise with the world!

They had another group with a similar philosophy. They felt they were free from sin's power; therefore they could do anything, even sin! This group was called the Nicolaitans, probably after its main teacher. This was within the church! This teaching emphasized the "FREEDOM" in Christ that Paul had taught but took it to the extreme.

This group basically pushed freedom above restraint! Like some today that talk about us being a FREE country, and that pornography, hate speech, etc. should be freely expressed. This freedom, however, can put you in bondage! Freedom without limits is NOT FREEDOM! When a man is released from prison, he is NOT free to now do anything he wishes. He is free to NOW obey the law by choice. If he uses his newfound freedom to break the law, he will find himself back in prison again! So it is with Christ. When we were set free from sin, we were freed so that we can KEEP GOD'S LAWS, not disregard them. To break God's laws will only send us back into spiritual bondage!

Christians that think they are so spiritually strong

that they can break God's laws are fools ... and will end up in spiritual bondage again! This was Paul's argument in Galatians, that we are free to serve Christ, not sin! It would be sad if the folks in this church encouraged each other to start living again like those in the community who were immoral. Christ's power to deliver would then be mocked!

"Repent, therefore!" is strong and emphatic language! The time to change was right then before damage occurred. It was very straightforward, not a debate on philosophy, but action! "Turn around" was the idea.

The tone is emphatic, and so must the action be!

The threat in the verse was that if they ignored dealing with these teachers of compromise, God would deal with them! How? The sword! (Remember the sword of IUS GLADII: the authority to kill at will by the governor, the symbol of the sword used for this!) The idea was God's judgment ... and even then, it would be to turn them around! We all know the biblical story of the shepherd and the wayward sheep. The shepherd breaks the leg of the constantly wayward sheep. It would not come when called and it was leading the other sheep to do the same. After healing, this sheep would be the model sheep, staying close to the shepherd, and thus leading the other sheep to do the same!

To those who heard, God promises "hidden manna!" This may have been soothing to those who had to break off social engagements at the local pagan temples where feasts were held in honor of the gods. To stand up to their faith meant losing out on the social scene, isolation. God promised them something better than material bread ... bread that would feed and nourish their spirit!

Not only would the "hidden manna" nourish them, but God's presence would make up for the loss of this world's presence. They wouldn't be alone!

The "white stone" may have been the "TESSERA HOSPITALIS," a white stone that was broken in half ... each party wrote their own name on their piece, which they would then exchange with each other. The meaning was: "a new name given them, that of their host." If they presented the piece of white stone with their host's name, they were entitled to everything their host owned! They literally had in their possession all that their host's name had ... like a major credit card without payments! These were only given out to the very best of friends ... because it gave them the right to everything you possessed!

Another possibility was the verdict stone, also a white stone used in courts of law. (Remember, this is the political capital — including court!) If a person was being tried by a jury or judge, they would be presented with one of two stones at the end of a trial … if declared not guilty, a white stone would be given them. If declared guilty, a black stone was given them.

The "new name" seems to push the first possibility more since the name of the host was only known by the one who held the stone. Jesus offers us, His best friends, a "TESSERA HOSPITALIS." All that is His is ours in Christ! Or He declares those who hear in the church "NOT GUILTY" if they respond! The call to compromise with this world and adopt their standards and ethics must be resisted by the church of Jesus Christ. We are to adopt standards of RIGHTEOUSNESS! The pressures to be like the world are real and powerful and sneak up on us if we are not on guard — watch and take inventory!

The pressures to compromise our faith are all around us! The church in Pergamum was in a gradual process of becoming "worldly." Unchecked, this process would dim their fire and witness for God. Already, they were tolerating in the church the teachings of indulgences. It wouldn't be long before the practices followed!

Which direction is your life moving in?

Frenzy of Feelings!

Revelation 2:18-29

"And to the angel of the church in Thyatira write: 'The words of the Son of God, who has eyes like a flame of fire, and whose feet are like burnished bronze.

"'I know your works, your love and faith and service and patient endurance, and that your latter works exceed the first. But I have this against you, that you tolerate that woman Jezebel, who calls herself a prophetess and is teaching and seducing my servants to practice sexual immorality and to eat food sacrificed to idols. I gave her time to repent, but she refuses to repent of her sexual immorality. Behold, I will throw her onto a sickbed, and those who commit adultery with her I will throw into great tribulation, unless they repent of her works, and I will strike her children dead. And

all the churches will know that I am he who searches mind and heart, and I will give to each of you according to your works. But to the rest of you in Thyatira, who do not hold this teaching, who have not learned what some call the deep things of Satan, to you I say, I do not lay on you any other burden. Only hold fast what you have until I come. The one who conquers and who keeps my works until the end, to him I will give authority over the nations, and he will rule them with a rod of iron, as when earthen pots are broken in pieces, even as I myself have received authority from my Father. And I will give him the morning star. He who has an ear, let him hear what the Spirit says to the churches.'"

Psychologists tell us that human personality is said to consist of four parts emotion and one part intellect. This means that when we make decisions, they are based on 80% emotional content and only 20% intellectual. Advertisers recognize this well-known fact by appealing strongly to our emotional nature ... and giving us little intellectual information.

Those who desire to be successful in dealing with others must consider the powerful dynamics of "feelings" if they hope to succeed. This doesn't make feelings evil, but it does demand that we try and balance better the dynamics of feelings and facts!

The same gifts of emotions that God has given us can become a vehicle of misguided power in our lives. We need the balance and checks of both. The church that ministers to the mind but not the heart will fail to move people to be passionate in their faith. The church that ministers to the heart but not the mind will drive the flock of God toward misguided and frenzied emotions, and where they end up will be anyone's guess!

The Bible clearly teaches that an overreliance on emotions can be dangerous and can create a cloud that obscures the paths that are clearly marked out for us to walk in God's Word.

Thyatira was a small, rural, blue-collar town ... very different from Ephesus, Smyrna and Pergamum, which were huge cities full of universities and powerful commercial centers. Ironically, this, the smallest of the seven cities, commands the largest letter ... showing God's value of something as very different from that of man's!

Many small trade guilds existed in this town ... a town well known for its textile and dye industry. Acts 16:14 tells us that Paul's first convert in Europe, a woman named Lydia, a dealer of purple cloth, came from this town. It is quite probable that Lydia had been a pioneer in planting this church and possibly acted as its first pastor. At the least, she was a leader within this church. This may help explain the reference to another woman who later claimed the role within the church as the "PROPHETESS." By this point in time, Lydia would have been dead.

This church had exactly the opposite problem from the church in Ephesus: Ephesus had great teaching but little to no passion ... they pursued a cold, emotionless doctrine. Thyatira had great passion but was weak on the doctrinal and teaching end. Like the other churches, this one was at an important crossroad ... their passions were driving them into ungodliness, and they were about to lose the good they had done and their many years of service to God in moral collapse. In the absence of some of the great leaders like Paul, Lydia, and other well-grounded teachers; other misguided teachers were attempting to redirect the passions of the church toward immorality while comforting the people with false-hoods, claiming that they could and should experi-ence Satan's temptations so they would be wise as to how Satan operates; that as long as they kept their spirit pure, it wouldn't matter what they did with their bodies!

The essence of allowing in creeping errors like this says that "God wants you to have fun. He doesn't want his people to be boring, so go to the temples of idols and party with the worshippers there. As long as you know they are only idols it won't hurt!" The emphasis was on pleasure ... not on truth!

Our society is a good mirror of this blue-collar church of the first century! It is portrayed in everything we see on TV and in print: It is our RIGHT to have fun ... the "pursuit of happiness." All too often, however, this is at the expense of character and unselfishness. Our motto goes like this: "YOU ONLY GO AROUND ONCE, SO REACH FOR ALL THE GUSTO YOU CAN."

In the path of this pleasure seeking, there are a host of broken-hearted people left behind: husbands and wives who are victimized by unfaithful spouses; children who are ignored so the parents can have more fun and get more; neighbors who are ignored unless there is some benefit to you; and people dying in sin because we need our recreation more than they need our witness! Thyatira, like many blue-collar workers, worked hard and played hard!

Jesus' introduction demonstrates the serious junction they were at as a church:

- "These are the words of the Son of God ..."

They had to be reminded of who God was!

- "... whose eyes are like blazing fire ..." He is watching, penetrating through their pretenses!
- "... whose feet are like burnished bronze." This is often a symbol of judgment! They will be held accountable for their actions!

The introduction is sobering and serious, perhaps severe enough to arouse their passions back to God. God knows the kind of language to use to get our attention. They needed their emotions stirred, so God accommodated them with moving language! The point Jesus was trying to make was that their condition had become serious enough to warrant a warning!

God, however, is sensitive to not overwhelm them with correction, so He begins with praise to arouse their passions to want to do right first! He begins with their strong points.

Their deeds: They were well known for their passion in service! These were not cold-hearted people. They could and were easily moved emotionally to feel the needs of others. They were not indifferent to other people, as is true with many blue-collar people! They had a string of wonderful responses to difficult circumstances and a reputation as caring and loving people!

Their "deeds" were not lacking because their motivation and passion were not lacking! Show me people who are passionate about anything, and I will show you a successful cause! Motivated people are the ones who change the world (for good or bad!).

Their love, faith, service, and perseverance are highly praised! This is their passion! They get high marks for the intensity of their sincere passion! They were quite the opposite of Ephesus in their passions!

God clearly states that their record indicates an INCREASING of works through the years unlike Ephesus whose works had decreased from lack of passion.

This was very much a PENTECOSTAL church with passionate worship and work! Their latter works were greater than their first. Their works are more now than at the beginning! In fact, their passions had not waned. They had grown!

Being a blue-collar town, it was a passionate community. If the church hadn't existed, they would have found it hard to reach their community!

"Nevertheless" (as the Word says) all was not well! Passion needs careful monitoring to keep it moving in the right direction. Their passion for people had created an interesting problem. Loving sinners created a toleration toward sinners who were bent on their destruction! They had come to tolerate a female leader symbolically called "Jezebel." It is unlikely that this was the woman's real name. Not many Jews would have honored the birth of a daughter with a name like this! It was not so much that this leader was a woman, because Lydia had played a similar role in this church's establishing. It was the direction this woman had taken them in her leadership!

Jezebel in the Old Testament was Ahab's wife who encouraged Israel to be passionate followers of Baal and to be passionate against the True God! She took whatever pleased her, even killing a man named Naboth just to give his vineyard to her whiney husband Ahab. Her passion was pleasure, her own!!! A high price would be exacted on anyone that took away her pleasure.

The teaching this woman had started in this church was very simple: To learn the limits of Satan's powers, they were supposed to go out and experience as much sin as possible. Unhealthy knowledge was the goal, but through undisciplined passion! She encouraged the Christians to participate at the local temples with the feasts celebrating demons so the people in town would identify with them, and by this build relationships with them. She told them not to worry what they did with their bodies as long as they kept their hearts right, thus entrapping many of them to wicked habits that they later couldn't break!

Satan still uses this lie. You can drink as much as you want, and you won't become an alcoholic! You can break God's laws of morality by sleeping around, and it won't hurt you as long as you really love the person (What a joke!). First, seek your own happiness, then you can help others be happy! This stuff is from the PIT OF HELL! SATAN IS A LIAR! You can't live on both sides!

This "Jezebel" and her teaching is very much still alive! Today, we have teaching that all "normal" people have sex outside of marriage, that it is o.k., that we need to have "fun" in life, i.e. throw aside God's laws in the process! Christians are falling for this mentality ... ignoring sin in their lives! We excuse sin by telling ourselves, "These passions are normal ... we can't help it!"

Passion directed properly is wonderful, a gift from God, but used against God's teaching, it is a death trap! Watch out for Satan's seductions! When passion becomes more important than what's right, we are on dangerous ground! When the church cannot grow without entertainment that tickles the passions in us, we are running close to sensationalism!

Don't get me wrong, I couldn't worship in a passionless church, but when I can't feel good about God or myself without an emotional high, I am in trouble! When I judge myself or others based on emotions, I'm heading for trouble! When I judge God on the basis of what I feel or don't feel, I'm in trouble!

When passion becomes too important, instability can result. We will only do what we are moved to do, not do what we know is right to do! The bed of suffering mentioned here is simply the consequence of living by emotions alone with no thought about the consequences of right and wrong. This will lead to severe consequences in this life! WE CANNOT AFFORD TO LIVE BY EMOTIONS ALONE!

Sensationalism will not build the kingdom of God ... spirituality will! It is easier to live by feelings than by faith but not wiser! "Hold on!" This was the message to those who were not just driven emotionally! They were asked to keep on the right path where they were at. God asked no greater burden from them! God was asking them to NOT SELL OUT! These saints were not unemotional, but they had their emotions guided by the clear teaching of God's Word. To them, God asks nothing more! Thus, God is not against emotions, but they must be wedded to truth!

In fact, God adds nothing to them because they had both! They were to hold on "until He comes," a promise of something better to come! The idea here is endurance: "does my will until the end," with the promise is that they will RULE! Those whose emotions serve them will rule. Those who are slaves to their emotions will be ruled over!

Then an interesting promise is made by God: "I will also give him the morning star." This is an obvious reference to Jesus! This is Jesus the Sovereign ruler of all! The promise is to receive Christ for all eternity, a great reward for keeping their emotions in check now!

They would not always understand everything in their life, and they would FEEL discouraged at times, etc., but the results of staying true to God would prove in the end most rewarding! And so it would be for those in Thyatira who stayed faithful. Their work may have seemed useless against the immoral society they lived in, but oh, the reward coming! Their work was uncovering the KINGDOM OF GOD!

"He that has an ear … let him hear what the Spirit says!"

This church had passion but lacked direction! Zeal without proper knowledge can lead into emotional frenzy. God asked nothing more of those in this church that had wedded zeal to proper teaching but warned those who were misguided emotionally!

Are your passions correctly focused by the Word of God?

Slow Death!

Revelation 3:1-6

"And to the angel of the church in Sardis write: 'The words of him who has the seven spirits of God and the seven stars.

"'I know your works. You have the reputation of being alive, but you are dead. Wake up, and strengthen what remains and is about to die, for I have not found your works complete in the sight of my God. Remember, then, what you received and heard. Keep it, and repent. If you will not wake up, I will come like a thief, and you will not know at what hour I will come against you. Yet you have still a few names in Sardis, people who have not soiled their garments, and they will walk with me in white, for they are worthy. The one who conquers will be clothed thus in white garments, and I will never blot his name out of the book of

life. I will confess his name before my Father and before his angels. He who has an ear, let him hear what the Spirit says to the churches.'"

Leonardo Da Vinci painted the masterpiece THE LAST SUPPER. He searched for someone to model for Christ. From a church in Rome, he located a chorister with lovely features named PIETRO BANDINELLI, a man he considered the perfect picture of Jesus.

After many years, the painting was still unfinished. All the disciples had been portrayed except one, Judas. A beggar from the streets of Rome was brought in with a face so villainous that people shuddered to look at him. Leonardo felt he would be perfect to represent Judas. After completing the painting, before dismissing the villainous bum, Da Vinci asked the beggar his name ... to everyone's shock, the beggar responded, "My name is PIETRO BANDINELLI!"

What had happened in the intervening years? This man had experienced a slow spiritual death, from a faithful churchgoer to a gutter bum. The degrading power of sin had gradually taken its toll, from the likeness of Jesus to that of Judas!

Our commitment to God's Word and His ways must be a continual process, even repetitious if we are to avoid the gradual effects and erosion of sin in our lives. We cannot afford to be off guard for a moment, lest sin's influence begins to erode our perception of sin. It can happen to anyone spiritually sleeping. This is the story of the church in SARDIS!

We must be always awake and on guard against an ungodly culture slowly wearing away our vigilance against sin. Even the most faithful saint can slowly lose their sensitivity to sin if they fail to keep a clear understanding of righteousness.

Sardis (may mean "Remnant") was a horribly ungodly and immoral city! The city boasted of its city's goddess, Cybele, a mother goddess that included some of the most immoral and perverted practices. Many can't even be mentioned without great embarrassment! A large temple dedicated to Artemis (Diana) was also in the area. Recent archeological digs have discovered that the CHURCH in Sardis was built ADJACENT to this temple! Their church building abutted the temple to Artemis ... making me wonder how the constant displays of orgies and immorality that were practiced at the temple influenced this church. Sardis was built on a steep hill, making the city almost impregnable. So secure was the feeling of its citizens that they often were lax in placing guards around the town; they didn't believe it was possible for any enemy to overtake them!

Ironically, their history records at least two major invasions that were successful, all because of their failure to place guards around the city. Their security was really a false security! Their great sense of security had created a mentality of looseness, and their efforts were spent on pleasures rather than on safety.

It was a very wealthy city. So much gold and silver were discovered here that they were the first city to mint gold and silver coins. The industries of the city included textiles, especially white cloth used for the temple participants! Worshipping at the temples required the necessary white garment. If it was soiled, you were expelled from the temple and excluded from any participation in the pagan rites! The steep, hilly area was a famous hangout for thieves, which helps to explain Jesus' warning about "coming as a thief" (not a reference to the second coming). One telling sign how bad the church at Sardis had gotten was no persecution of this church by any parties within Sardis! (While most of the other six churches mentioned were experiencing tough times from the local citizens, the church in Sardis seems to have no persecution from any source ... a good indication that they were not opposing local immorality.)

It seems the carefree attitude and the false sense of security of the citizens had also invaded the church. They were concerned with having a good time. It is also quite possible that the church was living off the reputation of the previous godly generation but was not engaging the issues of sin and degradation in its own day. "... You have a reputation of being alive, but you are dead!"

This church had a powerful reputation among the other churches ... but its present membership was nothing like the previous generation! The same false security of the city now existed in the church. They had let their guard down! Their deeds were pathetic and ungodly! They were DEAD!

This was God's description, not man's! They had gradually lost their way in the space of a generation. Their forefathers, the founders of the church, had created a reputation of real godliness, but now godlessness was ruling! They fully expected God's blessings to rest on them based on reputation, not on righteous living!

Like many people today in churches across America, they thought they could get to heaven on the reputation of a godly parent or godly leader. There are those today who think this way, too. They get baptized and associate with a denomination noted for being Christian and think that will get them to heaven ... but the reality of their own experience is void of any serious commitment to a Christian lifestyle! The appearance of being a Christian isn't the same as being one!

The church in Sardis was living a false spirituality, surviving off a reputation instead of righteousness. They had gradually decayed through the years. Like aging, it had happened so gradually that they were unaware of how far they had declined!

They had so relaxed themselves spiritually that they were asleep, so the first words of correction from Jesus are in the imperative: "WAKE UP!" The easy way out had made them lazy and sleepy; they needed to be startled awake! These Christians needed a good shake-up! Very little good was still going on in the church ... they had become inactive in ministry, going only through the motions!

The expression in this verse, "I have not found your deeds complete..." in the Greek means "NOT FULFILLED"... they didn't finish what they started ... possibly they were good at coming up with ideas but didn't carry them out. Like many Christians today, they might complain about this or that in the church but are themselves unwilling to do anything about those issues or needs! It is not enough to perceive truth ... it must also be practiced! They really needed to WAKE UP!

Like the city itself, the church failed to remember past invasions of enemies and so thought it was invincible. This church needed to remember its past and repeat it! In a reference they might understand, Jesus warns them that if they persist in believing they are so safe that they take no precautions against thieves ... He Himself will descend upon them: "I will come like a thief!"

This was not a reference to the second coming analogy used elsewhere ... it was a warning of judgment to come upon them suddenly if they failed to repent and change their ways, and soon! The city's failure to place guards due to their feelings of invincibility had allowed for the many thieves who hid in the hills to plunder houses from time to time. Just because their church had been founded by godly men did not mean that they would not be dealt with by God. They were nothing like their fathers! They needed to wake up!

"There are a few people in Sardis who have not soiled their clothes..." This is obviously a reference to the common practice of forbidding entrance to one of the local temples by anyone who tried to enter with soiled garments! If the local pagan temples excluded anyone with soiled white garments ... how much more the REAL God would exclude those who tried to enter with FILTHY RAGS OF SELF-RIGHTEOUSNESS! The emphasis here was not the concept of justification but the responsibility of the believer to take the necessary steps to keep clean! This is the human factor in sanctification!

It is a sad testimony that there were but a few left in the church that had not soiled their walk with God! This church was the opposite of most of the others ... in the others, God warns of going the wrong way by an emerging minority within those churches. Here, however, the minority was the godly group! This was a sad commentary on how far from their reputation they had drifted!

For those faithful, the promise is of white garments, the privilege of walking with God, and enjoying His presence in their daily walk! There were some in this church that had refused to walk the EASY path and were willing to stay on course no matter what!

Unfortunately ... there were too few willing to respond to this kind of challenge anymore! Yet a few existed in the church in Sardis who were men and women of God. I wonder how God would view our church today!? Would the godly in our church be the exception or the rule? Are we satisfied living off the reputation of the early years of our church? ARE we willing to have the same self-sacrificing courage and vision to reach out now? We are certainly more comfortable now than in the beginning, but are we as much committed?

To those who accept the challenge to live out their reputation, God promises two things: a. "dressed in white" — acceptance by God in HIS Temple! b. "to never have their name blotted out in the book of life."

This second promise is interesting. Is it possible that all men and women are listed in the book of life and are only blotted out if they fail to respond to Christ's invitation instead of the way we have commonly thought this out ... that of being written in when we believe? Perhaps this sheds light on the statement in Scripture: "Christ is not willing that any should perish ..." and that the sacrifice of Jesus was really for all ... but failure to respond then forces their name to be blotted out! Whichever, the promise is REAL SECURITY: to never be blotted out! Our name will be acknowledged by Jesus to the Father for those who are faithful! For those living off false security, this is a real promise of real security!

(It is not known whether this church responded or not. Historically, this church in Sardis existed until around 1402 A.D. when the old city was completely destroyed. The church, however, was never very prominent within this city as far as we know.)

It is never good enough for any church to exist off the past reputation of men and women of God! A church must ever keep its vision clear and its commitment hot! We cannot be God's church vicariously through the faith and godliness of others! We need a present experience ... and a present commitment to be a present witness!

A Powerful Church!

Revelation 3:7-13

"And to the angel of the church in Philadelphia write: 'The words of the holy one, the true one, who has the key of David, who opens and no one will shut, who shuts and no one opens.

"'I know your works. Behold, I have set before you an open door, which no one is able to shut. I know that you have but little power, and yet you have kept my word and have not denied my name. Behold, I will make those of the synagogue of Satan who say that they are Jews and are not, but lie—behold, I will make them come and bow down before your feet, and they will learn that I have loved you. Because you have kept my word about patient endurance, I will keep you from the hour of trial that is coming on the whole world, to try those who dwell on the earth. I am coming soon. Hold

fast what you have, so that no one may seize your crown. The one who conquers, I will make him a pillar in the temple of my God. Never shall he go out of it, and I will write on him the name of my God, and the name of the city of my God, the new Jerusalem, which comes down from my God out of heaven, and my own new name. He who has an ear, let him hear what the Spirit says to the churches.'"

What is it that determines the power of a church? The size of the congregation, the bigger the more powerful? NO! Is it the magnificence of the building? There are many beautiful structures we call churches, some costing millions of dollars but without the testimony of Christ in them! The variety of the programs offered? Activity doesn't prove anything. Large amounts of cash? No! Important people who are members?

In every one of the categories you could probably find both strong and weak churches. It must be something else that determines the power of a church!

The church in Philadelphia was small, the meaning of the phrase "little strength." They were not wealthy; they did not have important people of the community as members; and they were not mentioned for their many programs or beautiful, white steepled buildings.

WHAT IS MENTIONED is that they had done two things: "YOU HAVE KEPT MY WORD" (God's Word) and "HAVE NOT DENIED MY NAME" ... they had lived up to what a Christian should be. This is what makes a powerful church! They truly loved the Lord and each other!

God's Word teaches us how to be a powerful church. We must do two things: hold to God's Word without compromise and demonstrate God's love.

This small church's love for God and for His Word had caught the attention of the community, opening up many doors of opportunity for witnessing! It isn't always the large churches that draw people's attention to Christ! The vast majority of churches in the world are small!

THE ASSEMBLIES OF GOD (2006 figures) consists 34.4% of churches averaging 49 people or less in morning worship! (4,240 churches! Thus, more than a third of all our churches average less than 49 nationwide!) 28.7% average 50-99! (3,533 churches, meaning more than a fourth of all our church are from 50-100 nationwide!) This tells us that 63.1% average less than 99 in attendance! (7,973 churches, telling us nearly two-thirds of all our churches average less than 100 nationwide!) 83.1% of our churches average less than 199! (Total churches in 2006: 12,311)

Power comes from God's presence, not property, nor programs, nor prestige, nor personalities, nor provisions! The church must not see its size ... it must see the open doors God has given and walk through them. A door means nothing if it isn't used!

Though this church is said to have "little strength," it was also told it had an "OPEN DOOR that no one could shut!" This was because they had "kept God's Word" and "not denied His name."

This church had learned the secret to having God's power ... holding up His Word and really living it out in their daily walk! They had learned how to help each other! (This had to be a very "UPLIFTING" church!) A few people helping one another can really accomplish a great deal!

It was much easier living for Christ by "UPLIFTING" one another in faith and the Word! This gave them power beyond their numbers! This gave them unusual endurance capabilities! I couldn't make it spiritually without my brothers & sisters in Christ! We were never meant to go it alone!

God tells this church that in time their situation will reverse. For now, they might be made fun of or persecuted, but a day would come when they would be acknowledged as the focus of God's love! This would require great patience on their part and not to quit in the face of adversity! With patience, time would balance the scales of justice! Their patience waiting for God's justice would pay off great dividends ... NOW as well as THEN! NOW: It would give them great strength and opportunities for witnessing. THEN: God promises in the next verse to keep them from the terrible tribulation that will come upon the whole world! They would win in both time slots!

If we are patient, God really does protect His saints from tribulation, or at least through tribulation! (The Greek preposition "EK" can mean either "out of" or "through.") When the heat of God's wrath came upon the world, they would be protected by God for their faithful witness! Many see in this a promise of the rapture of the church. Jesus states clearly, "I am coming soon." History is marching toward an end that God Himself controls!

For those who patiently live out the Word of God, He promises that they will be prepared for that moment! They are instructed to "HOLD ON to what you have" lest they fail to have God's protection! It is not enough to have been saved; we must be holding on! This implies an active participation in waiting for Christ's coming ... to keep doing the right things until He returns! One of the signs of the last days will be those who will slide away from God and His Word. They will tire of being obedient and instead will choose to fulfill their own desires ("lovers of pleasure more than lovers of God")! The term "overcomer" is important to the concept of being "prepared."

To those who don't quit, to those who continue to "overcome," God promises to make them "pillars in His temple!" This was a powerful statement to someone from Philadelphia! Philadelphia was the city of many earthquakes! They had frequent earthquakes and occasionally they were big ones that nearly destroyed everything! A terrible one hit in 17 A.D., and many were afraid to return and rebuild. About the only thing left standing after the earthquake were the pillars of some of the temples and buildings! It was not an uncommon sight! What this demonstrated was that pillars were the only things that were left standing during an earthquake! The symbol stood for stability and durability!

They would stick out in the community as the real "PILLARS" no matter how few in number they might be or how limited their resources for spreading the Gospel! God was promising them a city from heaven, one not prone to destruction like the cities of earth! The whole picture here is that of PERMANENCE and STABILITY! This is God's promise to those who are prepared and overcoming! We need not fear the future, whatever comes, if we are walking with God!

We belong to Christ, His name, His city, His kingdom ... as overcomers we are secure in our position in His kingdom! No one else can lay claim to those who belong to Christ. We know who we are, and if we are walking with God, the world knows who we are! To those who overcome, He writes a NEW NAME on them ... HIS OWN NAME, meaning we belong to Him! Therefore, our position is safe. We will not be left to experience His WRATH. We are His Pillars even now!

This small church with its "little strength" (physically and perhaps financially) still had a powerful testimony, and because of this they would be standing when everything else fell! It wasn't their size. It wasn't their finances. It wasn't their prestige. It wasn't their educational degrees. It wasn't their programs. IT WAS THEIR EXAMPLE & THEIR LOVE!

This was a small church with a big heart! Their total commitment to God was unbreakable and without any compromise. God's promise to them was for many great opportunities and spiritual stability. Their witness one day would be acknowledged by even their enemies! God's final promise to them was to keep them from the tribulation coming upon the whole world!

This was a POWERFUL CHURCH! ARE WE?????

Mad Enough to Spit!

Revelation 3:14-22

"And to the angel of the church in Laodicea write: 'The words of the Amen, the faithful and true witness, the beginning of God's creation.

"'I know your works: you are neither cold nor hot. Would that you were either cold or hot! So, because you are lukewarm, and neither hot nor cold, I will spit you out of my mouth. For you say, I am rich, I have prospered, and I need nothing, not realizing that you are wretched, pitiable, poor, blind, and naked. I counsel you to buy from me gold refined by fire, so that you may be rich, and white garments so that you may clothe yourself and the shame of your nakedness may not be seen, and salve to anoint your eyes, so that you may see. Those whom I love, I reprove and discipline, so be zealous and repent. Behold, I stand at the door and

knock. If anyone hears my voice and opens the door, I will come in to him and eat with him, and he with me. The one who conquers, I will grant him to sit with me on my throne, as I also conquered and sat down with my Father on his throne. He who has an ear, let him hear what the Spirit says to the churches.'"

What is the worst thing that can happen to a church? Lack of finances? Lack of church activities? Lack of a pastor? (Sounds like a possible answer ... if you are a pastor!) Lack of facilities? Lack of committees ... on second thought!

It is none of the above! The surprising thing is this: The greatest problem a church can have is to feel that it needs nothing, thus it is self-sufficient.

The reason is simple. The church that has no needs becomes complacent. God ends up on the outside of the church, knocking to get in, the very picture we find in Revelation 3:20! (Often misquoted by Christians for salvation ... rather it is a picture of Christ and His church, with Christ on the outside hoping to be let back in!)

The text teaches us that God wants us to guard our personal and corporate life as His people from feeling so self-satisfied that we become spiritually lukewarm! Lukewarmness makes God mad enough to spit! Remember Jonah's lukewarm response to go and preach at Nineveh? Even the large fish "spat" him out!

Laodicea was probably the wealthiest city in the world in the first century! Since we live in the wealthiest country today, the parallels are likely to be strong. Its wealth was so great that in 60 A.D. when the entire city was leveled by a huge earthquake, it was entirely rebuilt without any financial help from Rome or any other outside source ... it was rebuilt with its own wealth!

The city was known for three major things: It had a vast and wealthy banking system (a New Testament Wall street!). It had a huge textile industry whose specialty was black wool cloth. It had a large and famous medical school which was famous for an eye salve called Phrygian powder.

All three of the things they were famous for and proud of are used by God to address the church's spiritual needs. The church was also extremely wealthy. It is stated so by God Himself! Yet, despite all its advantages, this church is the most condemned of the seven churches! It had a wonderful facility, as proven by archeological digs that have uncovered three buildings of the early Christian church. It certainly operated in a most businesslike fashion and did well financially! (The text states that they needed nothing materially!) The financial prowess of this church was such that any pastor or board would envy it! With all the businessmen and bankers in town, it was a church that no doubt was run in a top-notch fashion, YET ... God takes great exception to this church's spiritual condition! When God took their spiritual temperature, He pronounced them SICK!

The church in Laodicea had put great pride in what they possessed and not as much in being God's possession! The fires had dimmed in the light of self-sufficiency and an over-reliance on material things. While they weren't yet cold, they weren't hot, either. They were lukewarm and thus NO GOOD. Being labeled lukewarm was something they of all people could understand. With no natural water supply, the city had to pipe in water from six miles away. By the time the water reached the city, it was neither hot (from the naturally heated mineral springs at Hierapolis, used for its healing properties) nor cold (from mountain springs in the other direction). By the time the water reached the city, it was bitter and bland, and those who drank it often spit it out in disgust, leaving their thirst unrefreshed. It was well known the water was not good.

Likewise, their spiritual temperature was NOT GOOD! The church seemed quite impressive, with good finances, good business practices, a good name, probably well organized, with board members who were likely locally successful businessmen, or perhaps students from the medical school, and the well-educated. But looks were deceiving. Their self-sufficiency and arrogance had cooled their spiritual temperature!

The word translated "spit" is literally "vomit." God used a pretty strong word picture to make His point to this church! Jonah knew this experience quite well! His lukewarm commitment to God ended with a giant fish "vomiting" him out also. It was their usefulness ... or lack of it that God was upset about. They were existing just fine, but they were not useful! The bottom line of their problem stemmed from over-reliance on material things! (Not the "things" them-selves ... their security from those things!)

Like the town, this church had, through their 25-to 30-year history, acquired great wealth and great influence. With banks everywhere, and a huge textile plant, as well as a great medical university, this church must have been full of businessmen, bankers, college students and professors, supervisors, etc.! No doubt they felt on top of the world ... they were the church all the others could envy! They couldn't see how distorted their values had become. Instead of their abundance being accredited to God, they were taking the credit for it and relying on it instead of God! God tells them they lack the very necessities of spiritual life in terms they would well understand! They were "poor!" They were "naked!" They were "blind!"

They lacked the very three things they were most secure in, just in a different sense! So, they are counseled to open up their accounts and BUY NEW: "Gold refined in fire" ... spiritual wealth that comes only from going through trials; White clothes vs. the black clothes they were famous for (purity)! Also, to cover their nakedness ... nakedness was considered the most shameful thing that could happen to a person. (This says something about Christ's nakedness on the cross!) Eye salve was needed to correct their blindness problem, obviously a spiritual awakening so they could see spiritual things. The Holy Spirit is a healer! If they saw no need, they got lazy ... so God offered them what they DIDN'T possess!

God was offering them a different kind of wealth, the kind they were sorely lacking! These were the real necessities, not what they already possessed!

God explains His reason for such a harsh word to them ... He loves them! Love does not sit by while someone ruins their life … this is why parents discipline their children! God would not sit by and let them sink deeper into sin. Their values were taking them away from God. By loading up on this world's stuff, they were setting the stage for their own demise! God's Word to them was two-fold: a. "be earnest! (not half-hearted); b. "repent" (Turn around and head the other direction!).

This verse has been so misinterpreted through the years, often used as a salvation appeal for the individual. Its context, however, is quite different! The context is the church in Laodicea … not just individuals. The context is about the Christians in this church … not unbelievers. The picture is of Jesus who is OUTSIDE the church trying to gain entrance! How far this church had drifted!! Their wealth had created a self-sufficiency so great that it was as if Jesus was OUTSIDE the church trying to gain entrance again!

Jesus will not force Himself inside the church. He knocks, seeking entrance. If the door is opened, Christ promises to enter and share a meal with the church … or even an individual. This is interesting in that the meal spoken of here was the evening meal, the last and most important meal of the day. It was the last call for dinner before the darkness of night set in, a possible reference here to the end time tribulation period. Notice the promise includes mutual sharing, real fellowship with God. Mealtimes are one of the great places of sharing between people. It is here families share their mutual struggles and praises with each other, the events of the day and their lives together as family ... the context being the church. This passage offers us a great symbolic meaning for communion time.

The final promise is that of RULERSHIP & REST ... "on my throne" — rulership ... "sit" — the idea of completion or rest. The picture is of a church that will rule with Christ, their work finally complete!

Though we live as servants now ... we shall be rulers with Christ then! After all, we are King's Kids. Our great inheritance awaits our rapture, so store up your treasures where moth and rust will not corrupt them. We need to invest in HEAVEN'S SECURITIES & LOAN BANK ... FDIC approved! (Forever Deposited In Christ!)

This church had settled for earthly security and had fallen into mediocrity. Nothing will rob the church or the believer more, revealed in that this was one of the most condemned of the churches! A lukewarm church can make God sick to His stomach! There is no "ALL TEMPERATURE CHEER" in God's kingdom ... hot or cold, but not lukewarm!

There is no middle ground between heaven and hell, nor is there between commitment or lack of commitment to Christ! God's call is to be "hot" or "cold"... to be saved or not saved! There is no category of "sort of saved" or "sort of lost"! God finds lukewarmness unacceptable ... enough to make Him spit!

The Chorus

Revelation 4:1-11

After this I looked, and behold, a door standing open in heaven! And the first voice, which I had heard speaking to me like a trumpet, said, "Come up here, and I will show you what must take place after this." At once I was in the Spirit, and behold, a throne stood in heaven, with one seated on the throne. And he who sat there had the appearance of jasper and carnelian, and around the throne was a rainbow that had the appearance of an emerald. Around the throne were twenty-four thrones, and seated on the thrones were twenty-four elders, clothed in white garments, with golden crowns on their heads. From the throne came flashes of lightning, and rumblings and peals of thunder, and before the throne were burning seven torches of fire, which are the seven spirits of God, and before the throne there was as it were a sea of glass, like crystal.

And around the throne, on each side of the throne, are four living creatures, full of eyes in front and behind: the first living creature like a lion, the second living creature like an ox, the third living creature with the face of a man, and the fourth living creature like an eagle in flight. And the four living creatures, each of them with six wings, are full of eyes all around and within, and day and night they never cease to say,

"Holy, holy, holy, is the Lord God Almighty, who was and is and is to come!"

And whenever the living creatures give glory and honor and thanks to him who is seated on the throne, who lives forever and ever, the twenty-four elders fall down before him who is seated on the throne and worship him who lives forever and ever. They cast their crowns before the throne, saying,

"Worthy are you, our Lord and God, to receive glory and honor and power, for you created all things, and by your will they existed and were created."

The focus now changes. The outline of Revelation

was given clearly in the first chapter: things which you have seen; things which are; and things which MUST take place.

Interestingly enough, the beginning of revealing this future to John starts with a withdrawal FROM earth to heaven! We call this the rapture of the church, or as the Bible calls it, the "blessed hope" (Titus 2:13) of the believer. The anticipation of the rapture of the church should be in the heart of every Christian and in the uppermost consciousness of every church.

If we are not ready for the imminent return of Jesus, we are not ready for the future! The Scriptures teach us that the future is certain, that God has a wonderful plan and reward for His church, to catch it away to heaven.

The opening volley of the future begins with John being commanded to "come up here" — to heaven. The voice was "like a trumpet." The trumpet heralding this call heavenward sounds much like Paul's statements about the rapture of the church being preceded by a "trumpet" (1 Cor. 15:52; 1 Thess. 4:16) and Jesus' words that a trumpet will begin the process of His angels gathering together the saints in the last days (Matt. 24:31). John being snatched away here may well represent the church being snatched away at the beginning of the tribulation period, and it would fit with Paul's remarks that we are not appointed unto wrath (1 Thess. 5:9). The future in the book of Revelation thus begins with the "blessed hope" or the rapture of the church!

Rather than a doctrine of escapism, however, this hope has very practical purposes for the present. It encourages holy living in anticipation of an event, one that we can't possibly know when it will occur! 1 John 3:3 tells us: "Everyone who has this hope in him purifies himself, just as he is pure." Such a hope will keep us alert in the present! With the knowledge that we could be in Christ's presence at the "twinkling of an eye" (1 Cor. 15:52) we should keep focused in the present and how we live.

Notice that there is no hesitation in being translated to heaven: "… at once I was in the Spirit, and there before me was a throne in heaven …" Again, this reminds us of the language of Paul's description of what will happen to the believer when the trumpet of God sounds. It will be an instant change, like the "twinkling of an eye" (1 Cor. 15:52). No wonder we call this a "rapture" … it will be a joyous moment for every believer to be caught away and brought instantly into the presence of our Lord! There will be a whole chorus of worshippers gathered before Christ on that day. Will you be in their company?

John now attempts to describe the sight in heaven. Christ on the throne has the appearance of "jasper and carnelian." These two gems are interesting in that they were the first and the last gems on the breastplate of the High Priest in Israel, with the names of the first and last tribes of Israel inscribed on them (Ex. 28:17-21). This breastplate showed that the High Priest carried over his heart the entire nation of Israel … and Christ's appearance as of these gems perhaps represents Christ who has carried His people over His heart for eternity as our ultimate High Priest! This sight brought great comfort to John!

Jesus is also described by John as having "a rainbow resembling an emerald encircling the throne." The rainbow was the sign of a covenant, a perpetual one. The emerald green in color may represent God's mercy, thus a covenant of mercy. At this point, John discovers that he is not alone, that there are many others also around the throne. Heaven is not a lonely place! If you think you don't have to be a part of a church to be a Christian and worship God, you are in for a big surprise if you make it to heaven. Being around the church and worshipping with others will happen all through eternity, so you may as well get started on it here and now!!!

John was in good company! The 24 other thrones around Christ's throne may represent the 12 Patriarchs of the Old Covenant and the 12 Apostles of the New Covenant … again remember the symbol of the covenant over the throne of Christ. If so, this simply shows that the true church is one. All have been brought together from under both Old and New and made now as one … as indeed Paul said in Ephesians 2:14-15.

These 24 elders surely were not angels, but men who had great leadership roles like the patriarchs and apostles. These 24 elders are said to be wearing crowns – a symbol of reward, and no angels are ever said to have crowns or have earned them in any way. The only mention of creatures wearing crowns in the Bible are the places where it is promised that if we serve well and live well, we will be given crowns in glory, meaning these elders are not likely angels. They are likely redeemed saints. Their being dressed in white indicates purity … they were those who had been cleansed from sin. These garments were the ones they looked forward to, garments that will be ours one day, also! It was an exciting moment for this chorus of celebration!

John now hears thunder, reminding us of the times in the Old Testament when God spoke and it came forth like thunder and lightning. John was in the very presence of God. Unlike the Old Testament when Israel was fearful of God's thundering and lightning, John and the others are thrilled with God's presence, represented also in the "seven spirits" which simply mean God's perfect Holy Spirit.

The image of thunder also gives the idea of God's power and control. He is the conqueror! God's power and light were everywhere around the throne, and that is the only way John knows how to describe this sight. "Thunder, lightning, and seven lamps were blazing." The image here is clearly one of God's power and might!

John lived ready to go to His Lord ... and here he gets to see that moment!

John now introduces us to the "sea of glass, clear as crystal. In the center, around the throne, ..." In the Old Testament, the bronze laver was called "the sea" (1 Kings 7:23-25). It was the place between the tabernacle or temple and the altar of sacrifice ... the place of cleansing. John is describing the great "sea" around the throne, telling us that only those who have been cleansed can approach God's throne!

John describes four living creatures with six wings. Cherubim are described by Ezekiel as having only four wings, while Seraphim sport six wings, making it a bit of a guess to imagine these four creatures. The four creatures are depicted like a lion – Matthew's Gospel shows Jesus as the Lion of Judah; like an ox – Mark's Gospel shows Jesus as the sacrifice for man, the ox being a sacrificial animal; like a man – Luke's Gospel shows Jesus as the Son of Man; and like an eagle – John's Gospel shows Jesus as the one who connects us to heaven. Note that it is uncertain the exact meaning of these four creatures, but what they do is not uncertain. They cry out day and night, "Holy, Holy, Holy is the Lord God Almighty, who was, and is, and is to come."

These creatures, along with the rest in heaven, are in a constant state of praise over God's presence with them. Those who are cleansed from sins are worshippers! Knowing our sins are forgiven WILL MAKE US worshippers!

The eyes all over these creatures simply refer to the fact that they see God in front of them and man behind them ... perhaps a way of bridging the gap; and if this is meant, then the symbol of these creatures may be that of "priesthood" – those who stood in the gap between God and man. Note that they never stop giving "glory, honor, and thanks to Him who sits on the throne and who lives for ever and ever." The power of cleansing creates the power of worship! If we cannot worship God, it may be that we do not appreciate our cleansing or have not experienced it!

Note here that the 24 elders now fall down in worship before the throne, and they do something else. They take off their crowns and cast them before the throne of God! In this humble act, they recognize that their sacrifice cannot match Christ's sacrifice, that their reward pales in comparison! Throwing down their own crowns showed that they considered all that they had done to be nothing compared to now being in His presence. When we truly see Christ as He is and what He has done, our own self-righteousness and rewards will fall by the wayside!

The focus is ALL on Christ as they cry out in a chorus of celebration, "You are worthy, our Lord and God, to receive glory and honor and power, for you created all things, and by your will they were created and have their being." The chorus is sung, the work is done, the victory for the church is real! Christ alone gets the credit … and believers get to enjoy the benefits!

Are you ready to spend eternity with God? If the trumpet of God sounded right now, would you be left behind, or would you join the chorus of worshippers in heaven? The ticket is your sins being forgiven, with Christ as Lord of your life … have you taken this step of faith?

The first glimpse of the future in Revelation begins in chapter 4 with John being translated to heaven, away from the coming tribulation! The future starts with this "catching away" and the celebration around the throne of God for those who find themselves there! No dark moments are in the entire chapter — it is a chorus of confidence and celebration. The rapture of the church is indeed the "blessed hope."

Will you be "caught up" when Christ calls?

The Champion

Revelation 5:1-14

Then I saw in the right hand of him who was seated on the throne a scroll written within and on the back, sealed with seven seals. And I saw a mighty angel proclaiming with a loud voice, "Who is worthy to open the scroll and break its seals?" And no one in heaven or on earth or under the earth was able to open the scroll or to look into it, and I began to weep loudly because no one was found worthy to open the scroll or to look into it. And one of the elders said to me, "Weep no more; behold, the Lion of the tribe of Judah, the Root of David, has conquered, so that he can open the scroll and its seven seals."

And between the throne and the four living creatures and among the elders I saw a Lamb standing, as though it had been slain, with seven horns and with seven eyes, which are the seven spirits of God sent out into all the earth. And he went and took the scroll from the right hand of him who was seated on the throne. And when he had taken the scroll, the four living creatures and the twenty-four elders fell down before the Lamb, each holding a harp, and golden bowls full of incense, which are the prayers of the saints. And they sang a new song, saying,

"Worthy are you to take the scroll and to open its seals, for you were slain, and by your blood you ransomed people for God from every tribe and language and people and nation, and you have made them a kingdom and priests to our God, and they shall reign on the earth."

Then I looked, and I heard around the throne and the living creatures and the elders the voice of many angels, numbering myriads of myriads and thousands of thousands, saying with a loud voice,

"Worthy is the Lamb who was slain, to receive power and wealth and wisdom and might and honor and glory and blessing!"

And I heard every creature in heaven and on earth and under the earth and in the sea, and all that is in them, saying,

"To him who sits on the throne and to the Lamb be

blessing and honor and glory and might forever
and ever!"

And the four living creatures said, "Amen!" and the
elders fell down and worshiped.

The future unfolds with a dramatic moment in heaven. A scroll with seven seals represents the destiny of the earth and mankind ... and at first no one seems worthy to open the scroll. If no one is found worthy, what will the destiny of man be?

This is the question in the mind of mankind today. What will happen tomorrow? Will we be destroyed? Will we destroy ourselves ... will we be just a blip in this universe only to disappear again? Is the future certain and is anyone in control?

The answer is a resounding YES! Looking into the darkness of this world and the unseen future, we may wonder ... but if we look long enough, we will see a champion! John does not reveal the future that will one day darken earth until he has shown us the champion, the light in the darkness, and that is why this picture of our champion precedes the calamities on earth. The believer has confidence in the future, while the unbeliever does not! As Billy Graham famously said, he's read the last page of the Bible. He knows it's going to turn out all right.

The Bible confirms the certainty of the future. Christ is triumphant over time and eternity ... for the believer, the future holds great promises and celebration.

The scene in heaven opens with God on the throne holding in His right hand a large scroll sealed with seven seals. This scroll holds the destiny of the future ... and an angel cries out, "Who is worthy to break the seals and open the scroll?" The question reveals tension over the fate of the earth and mankind.

John says, "I wept and wept because no one was found who was worthy to open the scroll or look inside." This dramatic scene has John perplexed and fearful ... is he witnessing the sealed fate of humanity without even knowing what that might be? There is the sense that if someone could be found who was worthy enough to open this scroll that this same person would be the champion of man's destiny. There is a moment here of wondering ... at least from John's standpoint, hence his tears of fear.

John of course is thinking like a human. So many times man thinks he knows his future only to discover that he is not as much in control of it as he thinks he is!

Man's best attempts to know his future will always

fall short … man predicts a wonderful future of technological achievements that will eventually end all suffering and poverty … but history shows us that scientific advances only raise the stakes of tensions in the world, not diminish them. Man's power over his sinful nature is not strong enough to conquer it by his own strength … we need a champion to do this!

John's worry and pain is very real here … he weeps … the Greek word used here, "eklaion," is a strong word meaning "to wail, to sob, wail aloud!" John is distressed to think that mankind's future may be unknown and uncontrolled. Is even God able to control destiny?

Immediately, as John weeps, one of the elders in heaven speaks up and calms John by stating, "Do not weep! See, the Lion of the tribe of Judah, the Root of David, has triumphed. He is able to open the scroll and its seven seals." There is one, and only one who is worthy enough to open the scroll, who has control over the future. There is little doubt as to who this is. The "Lion of Judah, the Root of David" is none other than Jesus Christ Himself! The uncertain fear about tomorrow is answered in Christ, for He is worthy to open the seals, to control the future!

This is the repeated theme in the Bible. Jesus Christ is triumphant; he is victorious!

As John turns to look at the "Lion of Judah," he is surprised to see instead "a lamb, looking as if it had been slain!" It is surprising that a slain lamb could have the power to open the seal, but obviously, only one who had conquered sin could control the destiny of mankind, and this was the one who died for our sins, who overcame sin and death! This is Christ, both the Lion and the Lamb! It is His sacrifice as the "Lamb of God" that makes possible His rule over all things, for He has overcome! He is the "Lion of Judah" in heaven, but when we see Him, He appears to us also as the "Lamb of God which takes away the sins of the world." The angel saw Christ as the lion. John looks and sees Him as the lamb. John was a sinner saved by grace while the angel was not.

One would expect us to die for our sins, not almighty God. That God reversed this and died for us is incredible ... and unique among religions. In most religions, the gods expect their followers to pay for their sins, to somehow atone for them ... but in Christianity, God Himself paid the price to redeem us! Our future is wrapped up in the past sacrifice of Jesus Christ for our sins and in God who paid the price for our deliverance!

Notice in the text that the prayers of the saints (represented by the golden bowls held by those around the throne) are there before the throne of God. Those prayers we make are not lost. They find their way to God's throne ... hence we are told in Hebrews 4:16: "Let us then approach the throne of grace with confidence, so that we may receive mercy and find grace to help us in our time of need." They all sing a new song together: Worthy is the Lamb ... "God has purchased men from every tribe and language and people and nation."

John now sees those around the throne of God, and the crowd can hardly be numbered, for it is so great! John cannot count them all! The future is not dark. There is a great crowd in heaven, revealing that man's destiny is not an empty end. There will be scores of people in heaven who have accepted Christ as their Lord and Savior ... will you be in that number?

There is a continuous celebration of Christ's victory over sin and death! Rather than weeping, John is now celebrating ... thank God for a wondrous champion! When one realizes that God has made a way for us to be victorious over sin and death, one cannot help but burst out in worship! The scene here is one of "loud" voices of praise (in contrast to John's earlier loud weeping). "In a loud voice they sang, 'Worthy is the Lamb, who was slain, to receive power and wealth and wisdom and strength and honor and glory and praise!'" The focus has shifted from the sealed scroll to the one who alone is worthy to open it.

Where there had been tension at who could possibly be worthy enough to open the destiny of mankind, there is now relief with the only one who is worthy, Jesus Christ the Lord. They all break out in song. It is not a complicated song, nor one that requires a printed hymnbook. It is spontaneous and clear. "Worthy is the Lamb" is the song of the redeemed!

Everyone in heaven joins in the song ... heaven is now filled with joyful and intense singing, with worship of the Lamb of God. There is a champion in this universe, one who can be trusted with your future. His name is Jesus! There is no other god, no other way, no other champion!

Concern over the future has melted away into worship in heaven ... this is why we can worship today when facing a dark tomorrow ... we know that our destiny is in God's hands and that we will be triumphant in Christ! The sting of death is gone. The sting of sin is gone. No matter the circumstances of the present or the future, when we are in Christ, we can celebrate, for all of these things are under the control of our "champion."

A failure to celebrate when facing darkness is a failure to show confidence in our champion ... there is no excuse for failing to celebrate Christ's victory even in the midst of dark moments. Christianity is joyous faith, even when faced with difficulties! Joyfulness is the hallmark of Christianity. Even the Bible says, "The joy of the Lord is your strength" (Neh. 8:10).

John too is captured in the moment with worship and praise. There is one worthy in heaven to open the scroll ... one worthy of praise and worship, one worthy of taking away the sins of the world, one worthy to be champion of man's destiny. The only question left is, "Are you able to celebrate your future?" Is your sense of the future secure in the Lion of Judah, the Lamb of God that takes away your sins and secures your destiny? That confidence can start today, by accepting Jesus Christ as your champion, the one who has conquered sin and death, the one who alone is worthy to open up mankind's destiny.

Are there certainties in life? If so, who controls them? History is not stumbling toward an uncertain end. God alone controls the destiny of all things. The fact that Christ rules over time and eternity brings comfort to those who know Him as Lord, but discomfort to those who reject Him. If you want to be on the winning side, have Christ in your life. He is the only Champion!

Are you ready for tomorrow ... you can be!

The Calamities

Revelation 6:1-17

Now I watched when the Lamb opened one of the seven seals, and I heard one of the four living creatures say with a voice like thunder, "Come!" And I looked, and behold, a white horse! And its rider had a bow, and a crown was given to him, and he came out conquering, and to conquer.

When he opened the second seal, I heard the second living creature say, "Come!" And out came another horse, bright red. Its rider was permitted to take peace from the earth, so that people should slay one another, and he was given a great sword.

When he opened the third seal, I heard the third living creature say, "Come!" And I looked, and behold, a black horse! And its rider had a pair of scales in his hand. And I heard what seemed to be a voice in the midst of the four living creatures, saying, "A quart of wheat for a denarius, and three quarts of barley for a denarius, and do not harm the oil and wine!"

When he opened the fourth seal, I heard the voice of the fourth living creature say, "Come!" And I looked, and behold, a pale horse! And its rider's name was Death, and Hades followed him. And they were given authority over a fourth of the earth, to kill with sword and with famine and with pestilence and by wild beasts of the earth.

When he opened the fifth seal, I saw under the altar the souls of those who had been slain for the word of God and for the witness they had borne. They cried out with a loud voice, "O Sovereign Lord, holy and true, how long before you will judge and avenge our blood on those who dwell on the earth?" Then they were each given a white robe and told to rest a little longer, until the number of their fellow servants and their brothers should be complete, who were to be killed as they themselves had been.

When he opened the sixth seal, I looked, and behold, there was a great earthquake, and the sun became black as sackcloth, the full moon became like blood, and the stars of the sky fell to the earth as the fig tree sheds its winter fruit when shaken by a gale. The sky vanished like a scroll that is being rolled up, and every mountain and island was removed from its place. Then the kings of the earth and the great ones and the generals and the rich and the powerful, and everyone, slave and free, hid themselves in the caves and among the rocks of the mountains, calling to the mountains and rocks, "Fall on us and hide us from the face of him who is seated on the throne, and from the wrath of the Lamb, for the great day of their wrath has come, and who can stand?"

Jesus Christ's sacrifice on Calvary paid the price of redemption for sinful man, but it also did something else for sinful man. It secured judgment! Judgment and wrath are just as much a part of Christ's sacrifice as is His grace and love ... it matters which side of eternity you stand on, however, as to which one you will experience!

Many preachers today are happy to preach on Christ's grace and love, but the message of judgment must be preached, also!

Why does God reveal such horrendous portraits of judgment in the book of Revelation? It isn't just to satisfy a morbid curiosity about the future on our part. There is a purpose to these horrible details being revealed NOW. God reveals these things NOW as a warning about the reality of future judgment, not to satisfy our curiosity about future events. God's love saves from wrath those who repent, and God's love warns about wrath to come for the hardened heart. These revelations of the future serve as God's warning shots for the living NOW.

Frightening, YES! Completely avoidable, YES! … the point of this revelation is to warn us to avoid coming judgment, that there is NOW something we can do to avoid experiencing those events. If we know Christ, we will not experience His wrath, only His grace!

The reality of God's judgment is as much a part of the plan of salvation as God's grace. It all depends on where we choose to stand that determines which one of those two elements will be our experience. Now is our opportunity to choose grace!

You may have heard from your parents, "I'm warning you, if you don't listen, here is what is going to happen." This is like this chapter. John is shown the future calamities, and they serve as warnings of what will come should we neglect so great a salvation. Man will not stand before God and be able to say, "Well, I didn't know that this was going to happen." Love warns the disobedient, and it does not avoid detailing terrible consequences simply because a culture says it is uncouth or not politically correct to speak about God's wrath! In fact, we would have to question God's love if there was NO judgment on sin … this would not be a just God. How could He be a loving God if He avoided punishing the wicked? Parents who love their children are gracious when they obey and discipline them when they are bad … that is real love!

Christ is the one who begins to open the seals. Remember, He alone is worthy to open the sealed scroll.

How is it that such drastic actions must be taken at the end of time? Sin continues to plague humanity, and unless it is settled by our coming to the cross of Calvary, it will continue to yield its horrible fruit on people! These conditions are the natural results of sin left unchecked and unrepented of. Outside of Christ, sin is a ticking time bomb on humanity!

These harsh judgments are not unwarranted. God is not unfair. They are the result of deadly sin continuing its influence until it nearly destroys the human race — only God's intervention will prevent this.

Now we read about the "Six Seals."

The first seal shows a white horse with a rider who is given a crown and holds a bow … he is allowed to go forth and conquer the earth. This is not a reference to Christ. He is the one who opens the seal. It is a reference to allowing the Antichrist to conquer the earth during the tribulation period. Sin will finally have its master present in the person of the Antichrist!

The second seal shows a judgment of painful conquest. A red horse and the rider have power to take peace from the earth ... such is the master of evil and the price tag for following him.

The third seal is opened and a black horse with a rider holding scales comes forward, with power to produce famine on the earth.

The fourth seal reveals a pale horse and a rider with the power to kill a fourth of the population of the world. The tragic results of sin are death and destruction! This is the plight of sin unchecked and unchallenged.

The fifth seal is a bright moment during darkness, which I will talk about later.

The sixth seal has impact on all of creation ... sin's effects are far-reaching! The universe will be decimated by sin and the resulting judgment on it. It will shake the starry heavens and the earth below.

The seventh seal is found later in another chapter, so I won't deal with it here.

What a picture! It all seems so horrible. Why is a

loving God revealing such horrible things? Why this terrible description of the future? God is trying to use an "early warning system" here, showing us the ugly picture of judgment tomorrow and hoping we take heed TODAY! Such a horrible picture will hopefully make us rethink the desire to let sin rule in our lives, or in anyone's life ... and to spur us to evangelism! It is NOT illegitimate to use healthy fear to change bad behavior! Loving parents do this all the time to the children they love deeply! Fear can produce healthy changes. That is why our bodies have "fear" responses built into them that protect us from harm. Fear causes us to do things in response to the threat of harm.

In the middle of these six seals, there is a positive one, one that shows people responding to salvation, even at the cost of their physical lives. In this fifth seal, we find souls under the altar in heaven, people who gave their lives in order to serve Christ during this tribulation period. They are crying out, wondering how much longer they will have to wait, and Christ tells them only a little while longer, until all those who will belong are joined with them. This is a reference to others who will yet come to Christ during this horrible time.

God is in control. In the midst of evil, His light

shines! The only question in these seals is whether you live for Christ or for the Antichrist! Even as the full judgment of sin darkens the earth, God's grace is still at work. That is the powerful love of God. There is a way out, and His name is Jesus!

Now we confront the terrible price tag of sin, the separation that it produces between man and God. Notice that everyone who is a sinner, from kings to commoner, tries hiding in caves and among the rocks of the mountains to escape God, to flee from Him. Rather than worship the Lord and escape His destruction, they choose to escape God and worship the enemy!

This is the tragic picture of unrepentant sin, separation from God! Fear did not drive them to God, instead they ran away from God! If we harden our hearts against God, then neither good nor bad things will drive us toward Him. We can create such a hard heart that we only get worse whenever God attempts to warn us ... sinful impulses rule our behavior and make matters worse rather than better!

God is revealing this tragic future to help us steer clear of it. It is NOT JUST about tomorrow. It is very much about today! Billy Graham tells of his grandson in the aftermath of Hurricane Andrew. The young man was working to get food and water to the survivors when he saw a sign on one roof. It said, "Okay, God. You've got our attention. Now what?" This is God's point in the book of Revelation, to get our attention and make us say, "NOW WHAT?" And the answer to this is always the same: "Repent and be saved." These warnings are a loving God trying to say to us, "I love you. You can avoid all this pain. There is a better way."

What we see is a horrible picture of stubborn sinful man that causes him to flee from God's presence, and to choose to hide among the caves rather than come to the resurrection cave of Jesus Christ. Though we try to avoid angering people about the reality of damnation, it does exist! The final picture in this chapter shows wicked man calling for the rocks to fall on them, to crush them so they don't have to face God! This is the sentence of the lost … they will not be able to stand against God's righteous judgments, only those who have their sins forgiven.

Why do preachers fail to preach this side of God's nature? For fear of rejection by man. It isn't politically correct to speak about God's judgment anymore. It makes people uncomfortable, and they might not like you! People like "love" more.

Why should we preach this side of God's nature? Because it IS a part of the Gospel! Because people will be lost who don't hear it and turn from sin. Because God will judge the wicked. Because the wicked will face condemnation and everlasting punishment, the sentence of sin!

The other reason we study this chapter and look at these horrible events is so we will think about how we live in the present! How we live today can dramatically impact our tomorrows! We would be foolish to ignore this side of the Gospel message. Jesus warned of judgment to come, and so should we! It is not just scare tactics, but about turning from sin and toward God!

Christ is calling today … are you considering the price tag of what you are doing today, what price will you pay for how you live now? Today is the day of grace, and all this horrible judgment can be avoided, for Christ took our judgment on the cross of Calvary. If you accept Christ today, there remains no more judgment against you. We are then found in Christ and in heaven rejoicing with all the other angels and elders and saints! Why choose the painful side of the future when you can have the best, both now and then? While God's wrath awaits all those who reject Him, heaven awaits all those who turn toward Him.

Christ's work on Calvary has "good news - bad news" elements. Good News: The price tag for sinners has been made, and there is salvation for those who accept the sacrifice. Bad News: For those who reject Christ's sacrifice, there is only certain judgment awaiting, with permanent separation from God resulting. Why the dreadful vision here of calamities? So we can avoid experiencing them. There still is time — NOW! Turn to Him now to find a brighter tomorrow!

The Conversions

Revelation 7:1-17

After this I saw four angels standing at the four corners of the earth, holding back the four winds of the earth, that no wind might blow on earth or sea or against any tree. Then I saw another angel ascending from the rising of the sun, with the seal of the living God, and he called with a loud voice to the four angels who had been given power to harm earth and sea, saying, "Do not harm the earth or the sea or the trees, until we have sealed the servants of our God on their foreheads." And I heard the number of the sealed, 144,000, sealed from every tribe of the sons of Israel:

12,000 from the tribe of Judah were sealed, 12,000 from the tribe of Reuben, 12,000 from the tribe of Gad, 12,000 from the tribe of Asher, 12,000 from the tribe of Naphtali, 12,000 from the tribe of

Manasseh, 12,000 from the tribe of Simeon, 12,000 from the tribe of Levi, 12,000 from the tribe of Issachar, 12,000 from the tribe of Zebulun, 12,000 from the tribe of Joseph, 12,000 from the tribe of Benjamin were sealed.

After this I looked, and behold, a great multitude that no one could number, from every nation, from all tribes and peoples and languages, standing before the throne and before the Lamb, clothed in white robes, with palm branches in their hands, and crying out with a loud voice, "Salvation belongs to our God who sits on the throne, and to the Lamb!" And all the angels were standing around the throne and around the elders and the four living creatures, and they fell on their faces before the throne and worshiped God, saying, "Amen! Blessing and glory and wisdom and thanksgiving and honor and power and might be to our God forever and ever! Amen."

Then one of the elders addressed me, saying, "Who are these, clothed in white robes, and from where have they come?" I said to him, "Sir, you know." And he said to me, "These are the ones coming out of the great tribulation. They have washed their robes and made them white in the blood of the Lamb.

"Therefore they are before the throne of God, and

serve him day and night in his temple; and he who sits on the throne will shelter them with his presence. They shall hunger no more, neither thirst anymore; the sun shall not strike them, nor any scorching heat. For the Lamb in the midst of the throne will be their shepherd, and he will guide them to springs of living water, and God will wipe away every tear from their eyes."

John reveals the darkness of the tribulation period to be a time of great suffering and evil. YET, during even this great darkness, he also reveals the power of the Gospel ... a huge multitude find Christ as their Lord and Savior!

This is the picture of the Gospel all through the ages, even in the darkness of the age to come. Whenever the world becomes a dark place, the light of the Gospel continues to shine. Satan cannot overwhelm the light of the Gospel. We discover hope even in the darkness. As Christ's coming approaches, the darkness is penetrated by the power of the Gospel.

There will be a multitude who will respond even as the end approaches. The devastation of Satan will cause some to look for a better solution, one they will find in Christ. Why does God allow suffering and tribulation in this world? So we will turn from darkness toward His light. Satan is not in control. God is! The Bible clearly teaches us that at no time will evil triumph over good, even though for a time it may appear that way. God's love will find a way to reach the lost, even in the darkest of times!

God's plan covers the whole world, indeed everything! "After this I saw four angels standing at the four corners of the earth..." The idea here is that God is concerned about the whole planet! God's love and concern are not limited to only a portion of the planet or a specific period of time ... His love covers all time, all places. God does not abandon His creation.

It is God's nature to care ... even when man turns his back on God! His creation may turn away from Him, but God does not turn away from His creation. Even during the tribulation period on earth, God is watching out for the whole planet. Satan does not have free reign! Satan believes he has triumphed, that he is in control ... but he is deluded by his own pride. Such pride of self-importance is the basis of all sin. Such independence from God is what makes a man believe he is in control, that he is his own master. Such arrogance is at the root of all sin!

While those on the earth think they are ruling, however, it is really God who is in control of all things!

God limits the damage on the planet, even when

the Antichrist is in full power! The foolishness of pride is that we believe we are taking care of everything by our own strength. The truth be told, God is fully in control of what is happening in the universe. There is no time when His hands are tied. God's purposes for establishing His kingdom will not fail ... this is the confidence of faith. We do not have to fear the future. God will always be in control of it. Even the greatest wickedness of man's scheming cannot undo or block the purposes of God.

This is the aspect about God that the world has a hard time swallowing ... that God permits man to express evil ... and yet such expressions do not undermine God's will for the future! God uses such painful times for positive results in those who walk by faith!

The amazing power of grace is the ability of God to take what is painful and produce spiritual wealth from it. Even in the tribulation period (as in all times of tribulation!) God's powerful grace is at work to transform what would appear to be losses into gains!

As God did with Job, He continues to control the powers of Satan even in the worst moments of history. It is hard to see this during such times of darkness, however! It is not easy to find God's purposes within the single incidents of life. It is clearer when we view the entire scene of history! God considers the big picture and is always at work for our good, even when we can't see or feel any good in our moment of darkness.

We must guard against the despair that comes when we can't combine all the works of God into a single unit … and trust Him even in the midst of the dark times. One day we will appreciate the whole picture and understand His purposes.

God will never lose control of mankind … even when Satan is at his height of power … God is still the master! If this is true at the end of time, it is also true right now!

God's plans are built around His love for His people! Even in the worst of times such as the tribulation period, we see God's protective hand around those who belong to Him! God will preserve a remnant … as He promised to Abraham.

We see God's faithfulness to His promises to Abraham, where he was assured that there would be a Jewish remnant saved in the tribulation period. The figure doesn't have to be taken literally as 144,000 … this multiple of 12 may simply indicate God's perfection. He will save perfectly those who turn to Him from Abraham's seed. One interesting note on the list of 12 tribes is that the tribe of Dan is missing completely ... Manasseh is listed, and so is Joseph, to make the number total to 12 tribes, while eliminating the tribe of Dan. Dan was noted for its constant idolatry, and this may be why it is left out ... or another theory is that the Antichrist comes from the tribe of Dan. The important feature here is that God will redeem those who come to Him, even in the times of humanity's deepest darkness! There will be hope even as the Antichrist rules over the earth ... Christ will still seek to save the lost. Those who are sealed by the Antichrist will be lost, but Christ will also find a remnant to seal, those whom He will save. This vast group of Jewish believers will become the witnesses of Christ's Gospel in these last days of tribulation.

The good news in this evil time is that this remnant of Jewish believers takes the Gospel to the whole world, and there will be a great host of people saved from every tribe, every nation, and every tongue.

God's love and power has not diminished under Satan's terrible attempts to destroy God ... in fact, the saving power of God is still very much at work in the world. There will be those who realize that their only hope is in Christ! Sometimes it takes this drastic darkness for men to realize their need of a savior!

If Christ can be found in the midst of horrible evil, surely He can be found right now! Do you feel alone, empty, deserted, struggling in the darkness and wondering where God is? He is here, right now, waiting to come in ... He responds to faith, so trust in Him and His purposes even when the outcome looks bleak. God cannot disappoint; indeed, He is faithful!

Does this mean that everything goes well after finding Christ? Many of these believers will suffer martyrdom for accepting Christ. Comfort isn't the goal of faith. Commitment is! In the face of persecution and even death, there will be men and women who will stand up to be counted in their faith ... their comforts in this world will be secondary to their commitment to Christ for eternity. Living for God is not a matter of being pain free in the here and now, but a commitment of our lives to Christ NO matter the present cost.

When the elder asks John who all these believers are and where they come from, John simply responds, "Sir, you know." The elder then identifies the blood-bought saints: "These are they who have come out of the great tribulation; they have washed their robes and made them white in the blood of the Lamb." Notice the elder is careful not to say that they have washed their own robes ... they are washed only by the blood of the lamb. Even during great tribulation, God's plans are at work. God is in control of all things

... working out everything for the sake of His people.

God has a plan for your life. If you come to Him, He will not abandon you. He will not allow darkness to overtake your life. He will be there during the greatest tribulation of your life. Why not trust Him? You don't have to wait until tomorrow!

John concludes this parenthesis between the sixth seal and the seventh seal with this wonderful picture of the redeemed of God worshipping Him, even those who have come through the great tribulation. The final outcome for believers is one of great celebration and victory. Though beaten and battered on earth, these saints now reside in heaven with the reward of the righteous. Not all the scales of justice show up in the here and now ... but faith will NOT go unrewarded in eternity.

The former pains and sufferings will disappear in heaven. Knowing this NOW helps us to endure what comes NOW AND LATER. It is this knowledge that gives our present existence meaning ... and with meaning we can handle just about anything that comes our way! There will come a time when all sorrows will be erased, when all the sufferings of this world will pale in comparison to the rewards of eternity. When tough times come, even when there seems to be no justice now for sorrows suffered, remember that God doesn't always settle the accounts on this side of eternity. God takes notice of everything, and He is always in control ... we need not despair even when the forces of darkness are pressing in on every side ... the final outcome is victory for the saints of God!

In the midst of tribulation, we would expect a scene of devastation, yet John shows us a picture of God at work in the hearts of men and women who respond to Him. Even in a horrific time, God's plan and purposes are being fruitful to win the lost. The power of the Gospel is greater than the power of Satan!

Will be you be among that number celebrating around the throne of God? YOU CAN BE!

The Contrasts!

Revelation 10:1-11

Then I saw another mighty angel coming down from heaven, wrapped in a cloud, with a rainbow over his head, and his face was like the sun, and his legs like pillars of fire. He had a little scroll open in his hand. And he set his right foot on the sea, and his left foot on the land, and called out with a loud voice, like a lion roaring. When he called out, the seven thunders sounded. And when the seven thunders had sounded, I was about to write, but I heard a voice from heaven saying, "Seal up what the seven thunders have said, and do not write it down." And the angel whom I saw standing on the sea and on the land raised his right hand to heaven and swore by him who lives forever and ever, who created heaven and what is in it, the earth and what is in it, and the sea and what is in it, that there would be no more delay, but that in the days of the trumpet call to be sounded by the seventh angel, the mystery of God would be fulfilled, just as he announced to his servants the prophets.

Then the voice that I had heard from heaven spoke to me again, saying, "Go, take the scroll that is open in the hand of the angel who is standing on the sea and on the land." So I went to the angel and told him to give me the little scroll. And he said to me, "Take and eat it; it will make your stomach bitter, but in your mouth it will be sweet as honey." And I took the little scroll from the hand of the angel and ate it. It was sweet as honey in my mouth, but when I had eaten it my stomach was made bitter. And I was told, "You must again prophesy about many peoples and nations and languages and kings."

The second coming of Christ to most people is nothing more than a fantasy. To some it is nothing more than religious nonsense. Modern man may wonder how sophisticated and modern Christians can really believe that Jesus is coming again, or that there will be a tribulation period that will wreak havoc on this planet.

Yet, as we get closer and closer to the second coming of Christ, such ideas hardly seem fanciful. The closer to Jesus' coming, the less fanciful the prophecies about the future will appear to be. Even in the world there have been those times when things that sounded fanciful at one time became quite credible later on ... what seems incredible today becomes tomorrow's facts. The world has frequently had to say, "Whoops, guess we were wrong after all." Those who now believe the second coming of Christ is a fanciful idea will one day have to say, "Whoops, guess we were wrong after all." But what tragic consequences will arise from their error.

In 1919, the New York Times derided an article written by Dr. Robert Goddard, the man called the Father of Modern Rocketry. In the article, Goddard suggested that a rocket could carry a payload to the moon. The Times said that Goddard didn't have "the knowledge ladled out daily in high schools." Forty-nine years later, the Times published a retraction, admitting that they were wrong and Goddard was correct — as Apollo 11 circled the moon!

Up until this century, it was thought that the 200-million-man army mentioned in Revelation that comes from the east must be a "spiritual" or "symbolic" number ... how could this be real, BUT today China alone can easily put this many men in uniform (Rev. 9:16).

Until the middle of this past century, many "experts" thought the regathering of millions of Jews back to Palestine to again become the nation of Israel was nothing more than a "spiritual" concept ... though the Bible said it would literally happen at the end of time (Ezek. 37).

Zechariah and Ezekiel describe a horrible force so great that people's skin will fall off from a blasting heat that is so sudden that their eyes will melt in their sockets while they still walk about. It seemed too farfetched ... until this century when the atomic bomb was dropped, and this was the EXACT description by survivors who saw those exposed to the blast ... still living ... and walking about just like this (Ezek. 39:6; Zech. 14:12).

What once seemed too fanciful to believe is quite literally possible today! Jesus is coming again!!! This is not a fanciful delusion. It will be fact! The Bible clearly teaches that there should be an urgency in telling others about Christ's salvation, that Jesus is coming soon!

John sees a mighty angel again ... probably the same one he saw in 5:2. The "rainbow above his head" shows that God never forgets His covenantal promises, of which the rainbow was a symbol. The "fiery pillars" for legs remind us of the pillar of fire that always went with Israel through the wilderness showing God's presence among them.

This angel held a "little scroll" or little book ... we don't know the contents, however. The fact that the little scroll "lay open in his hand" however would indicate that this was to be revealed to John. It was, after all, "open." There seems little doubt that this "little scroll" contained judgments of some kind, perhaps the judgments of the seven thunders ... being "little" it may have meant that this was a part of a larger revelation.

The "seven thunders" remind us of the similar "seven seals, seven trumpets," and the coming "seven bowls" ... all of which are judgments on sinners, so it seems consistent that these "seven thunders" would also be a set of seven judgments.

The "seven thunders" utter their judgments, and John is about to write down what they say, when a "voice from heaven" tells him NOT to write it down. These judgments are to be kept secret until the day they are visited upon the earth. While open to John, they are closed to us! It would be foolish to speculate as to what they are, but no doubt they are horrible, as are the "seven seals, seven trumpets," and the "seven bowls" yet to come. Perhaps they are of such a nature that one could guess the time frame from them, so they remain hidden. We just don't know what the thunders said!

What God is doing here ... is giving another final warning so that mankind cannot say they have not been warned! Tragically, too many today think that life will just continue on with them always in control ... the arrogance of man's heart in thinking that he has everything under his control for the future, that the need for God doesn't exist! We fail to realize that only God controls the future ... we really have little power for very little time!

Though what the "seven thunders" said is not revealed, what they say will happen will happen! A sense of urgency is here, as the angel lifts his right hand toward heaven and says, "There will be no more delay!" There will be no more time to put off a decision for Christ, to avoid the judgments on sin. There is a fixed time for such a day of judgment, and it will surely come as God directs.

How we like to put off dealing with things! This is almost a way of life today, to put off until tomorrow dealing with something that we really should deal with now. This is the way many people respond to the message that Jesus is coming again ... they say that one day they will seriously think about the claims of Christ ... maybe when they are older. Jesus, however, will not delay His plans despite how we feel! So many of us always think there will be a way to postpone such serious decisions ... yet not even the most powerful of human beings can change what is inevitable!

The "mystery of God will be accomplished," the angel states ... no more delay, just as God had "announced to his servants the prophets." No wonder the Bible states so emphatically in 2 Corinthians 6:2: "... I tell you, now is the time of God's favor, now is the day of salvation." We cannot assume there will be another opportunity later. There will be a day when the angel of God will declare, "No more delay!"

The same voice from heaven now speaks to John again, and this time it asks something strange ... for John to "Go, take the scroll that lies open in the hand of the angel who is standing on the sea and on the land." Notice that the angel doesn't GIVE IT to John. John is asked to GET IT himself. John is being asked to be responsible with the scroll containing God's Word. No angel will force him to take it. He must get it for himself from the angel.

God has chosen to ask us to take His Word ... He does not force it upon anyone!

Notice too that God says, "It will turn your stomach sour, but in your mouth it will be as sweet as honey." There is a contrast here ... God's Word is sweet to John's taste, but sour as it settles in him ... the invitation is to receive God's Word willingly ... and to do more with it than just have it sit around our homes ... it is to be absorbed by us, to become a part of us!

The hardest thing about sharing the Word of God with others is that we are afraid it won't do any good ... but we must remember that our responsibility is to share it. The results are up to God! Sometimes it will produce nothing ... but maybe only for the moment. It later might produce life in the hearer ... we must not base our responsibility on what we think might happen! John was not told what kind of results would come from his taking the scroll ... just that he was to take it and consume it. Whether it changed mankind or not, John was to obey!

We have a responsibility to tell others about Jesus Christ ... and that He is coming again and that all sin will one day be judged. We are not responsible for people's responses, but we are responsible for telling them! We can never know how people might respond, either initially or later ... but they CAN'T RESPOND if they don't hear!!! But they MAY RESPOND if they do hear! How faithful have you been to tell others about Jesus?

What did God mean when He said that the scroll John ate would turn "your stomach sour, but in your mouth it will be as sweet as honey"? For the believer, the Word of God is sweet. Even the judgment against sin is sweet to one who is redeemed from sin, for he is free from judgment! BUT ... a believer who loves God should also love the world ... and when it is digested (or understood) that God's judgments will come against the unrighteous, it should make us sorrowful to realize that so many will suffer judgment. When we realize all those who will suffer but don't have to, it should not sit well with us, either!

It made John sick to his stomach to realize that God's Word would bring judgment against those failed to receive Christ. John experiences no delight in sinners being judged ... though the Word was sweet to him, he is pained over those who are lost in sin and now find themselves experiencing God's judgments. This should be our heart too ... rejoicing over our own salvation, broken over those still lost. We cannot become satisfied with just our own salvation.

Do others know we are Christians, that we are redeemed? The fate of millions may well be in our hands ... and though we find our salvation such a sweet thing ... we must allow ALL of God's Word to settle in our hearts so that we see how tragic it will be for those who are lost ... our gut reaction to the lost condition of sinners should cause us to be uncomfortable enough to actively work to reach the lost. John's experience of the bitterness reflects the true heart of a godly disciple ... he cannot be fully comfortable knowing what is coming to those who don't know Christ, even though the Gospel tastes sweet to us who know Him. What about us today? The events of the book of Revelation are GOING TO HAPPEN one day, perhaps soon ... what are we doing about those who are lost in their sins?

Notice God's last statement to John in Revelation 10:11: "Then I was told, 'You must prophesy again about many peoples, nations, languages and kings.'" John's call was to preach! This is the good news ... that today is still the day of salvation! John's message would go forth to all the nations, to all peoples, in all languages ... we can be a part of this today, still!

We are fortunate that God has revealed the future to us. This way we realize how important and necessary it is that we tell as many people as possible the good news that Jesus Christ saves. Revelation should inspire us and produce concern, godly concern for the lost. While we may find the future events of the book of Revelation sweet, knowing we will be with Christ ... we must also let it settle in our gut that there will be many who will experience God's judgment ... and let this move us today to reach the lost. It is just such a contrast that gives us a sweet appreciation for our salvation and the impetus to reach out to others still lost.

John is shown some of the final warnings and judgments, and he is told that the end is near. No more delay! Such news is both sweet and bitter, sweet to him as a believer because his full reward is coming, and bitter because so many will be lost. Does the soon coming of Christ cause us enough concern to proclaim Christ's salvation?

How are you responding to God's revelation? What are you doing about the future today, in both your own life and in the lives of those around you?

The Calling

Revelation 11:1-14

Then I was given a measuring rod like a staff, and I was told, "Rise and measure the temple of God and the altar and those who worship there, but do not measure the court outside the temple; leave that out, for it is given over to the nations, and they will trample the holy city for forty-two months. And I will grant authority to my two witnesses, and they will prophesy for 1,260 days, clothed in sackcloth."

These are the two olive trees and the two lampstands that stand before the Lord of the earth. And if anyone would harm them, fire pours from their mouth and consumes their foes. If anyone would harm them, this is how he is doomed to be killed. They have the power to shut the sky, that no rain may fall during the days of their prophesying, and they have power over the waters to turn them into blood and to strike the earth with every kind of plague, as often as they desire. And when they have finished their testimony, the beast that rises from the bottomless pit will make war on them and conquer them and kill them, and their dead bodies will lie in the street of the great city that symbolically is called Sodom and Egypt, where their Lord was crucified. For three and a half days some from the peoples and tribes and languages and nations will gaze at their dead bodies and refuse to let them be placed in a tomb, and those who dwell on the earth will rejoice over them and make merry and exchange presents, because these two prophets had been a torment to those who dwell on the earth. But after the three and a half days a breath of life from God entered them, and they stood up on their feet, and great fear fell on those who saw them. Then they heard a loud voice from heaven saying to them, "Come up here!" And they went up to heaven in a cloud, and their enemies watched them. And at that hour there was a great earthquake, and a tenth of the city fell. Seven thousand people were killed in the earthquake, and the rest were terrified and gave glory to the God of heaven.

The second woe has passed; behold, the third woe is soon to come.

This chapter in Revelation takes us from the middle of the tribulation period to near the end of it. This covers the last 3½ years of the seven-year period.

No period of time in the earth's history will be darker or more sinister than this period of time. Evil will appear to triumph completely over righteousness. Yet, even in the worst of times, God has servants ready and willing to preach the Gospel of Jesus Christ. No matter the situation, the Gospel marches on ... as does the church!

The preaching of the Gospel has occurred at the worst moments of human history, and it will be no different in the tribulation period. We must never underestimate the power of God's Word, either now or in the future. The Bible teaches us that God's calling to tell others about Christ will not cease until the final days of time. It is a call we must all answer during the time we live.

As John takes us to the midpoint of the tribulation, we see conditions deteriorate. The Antichrist has just desecrated the temple by setting up his own image in it. The Jews now realize that the Antichrist is not their long-awaited messiah. This event dramatically changes the atmosphere on the planet, and we enter the "great tribulation" — a time of unparalleled evil, and judgment ... And yet ... God still desires to have the message of salvation preached! God will raise up in Jerusalem two witnesses who will testify for Him to the Jews and the world. These two witnesses will preach for the last 3½ years of the seven years of tribulation of judgment on sin — indicated by their wearing of sackcloth.

God doesn't need a vast army, nor does he need modern technology ... He just needs two men who will speak up for Him. Why two? The Bible says that every matter must be established in the mouths of at least two witnesses. God doesn't need a lot of "stuff" to accomplish His purposes, just obedient people who will speak His Word.

Notice that though the days are full of evil, these witnesses for Christ are given God's power to witness. Nothing can stop them. God has ordained them to do the work of ministry and not even Satan can hinder them or prevent them from preaching the Gospel. This raises an important point: If Satan cannot prevent their ministry even when he appears to have full control over the earth, then we can be sure that he cannot prevent the preaching of the Gospel today either! This means ministry CAN happen if we are willing to be used.

The two witnesses have the power of Moses and Elijah: a. to shut up the heavens from rain, or to loose the rain; and b. to have plagues hit the earth like they did on Egypt.

There would be supernatural manifestations following their preaching ministry ... a similar promise in the New Testament for believers today! We can expect God to do great things when we preach His Word. God will confirm His Word with signs following (Mark 16:17).

They are committed to preaching despite the pressures! While not always the popular thing to do, preaching the gospel of Jesus Christ is the mission of the church, and thus the responsibility of every member of the body of Christ. The two witnesses preach with the Holy Spirit's power and enablement. Certainly, the image of these two witnesses as "two olive trees" would indicate that God's Spirit was their supply, as olive oil is often used as the symbol of the Holy Spirit. If we had to depend on our abilities, the Gospel would surely fall away, but God promises His power so that we are sure of success.

The preaching of the Gospel is not dependent on our abilities. It is anointed by God's Spirit. Therefore, nothing will stop it! It never returns void! Isaiah 55:11 says: "So is my word that goes out from my mouth: It will not return to me empty, but will accomplish what I desire and achieve the purpose for which I sent it."

Notice here that God's plan includes a witness to the whole world, that the Gospel will be fully preached ... ONLY then is Satan allowed to kill these two witnesses ... only after they FINISH the task given them by God. Satan in not in control, GOD IS! The lives of these servants are protected until they have accomplished God's purposes in their lives. We must not live in fear. God's hand on our lives is so powerful that only when we have completed God's task does our time on earth end.

Notice that the world so hated these two men that they celebrate and send gifts to each other after they are killed. The world was critical of their message ... which no doubt included preaching judgment! They did not hesitate to tell the whole truth, despite how popular they were ... or how popular they weren't!

If we are afraid to witness because we don't want people to think badly about us, then we are letting people go to hell! It is too important to ignore ... and we need to realize that even if our message isn't always well received, it is needed! The proof of the message by God's two servants in Revelation is witnessed by the world when these two witnesses are resurrected back to life, and then they are raptured to heaven. In the end, the message we preach will be authenticated by God's power to raise the dead.

This was the proof of Jesus' claims and message ... when He arose from the dead, it settled the issue of whether He was God or not! These two servants, though despised by the world, are honored by the Lord ... and they are raised back to life as evidence that they were sent by God with the correct message. Satan could do nothing about this, either! It simply states that when God raised them back to life and took them to heaven, that "their enemies looked on."

As the witnesses are caught up to heaven, a great earthquake causes a tenth of the city to collapse ... killing 7,000 inhabitants. The result of this causes fear to strike the survivors, and they did something interesting here. They "gave glory to the God of heaven." Have they finally turned from their sins as they witnessed God's power to raise the two witnesses back to life and take them to heaven? Has God's power in the earthquake made them rethink their relationship with God? The answers to the above questions are a resounding NO!

While they are briefly willing to offer glory to God ... they are not willing to repent of their sins! Their last-minute decision to glorify God does not represent a real change of heart, just a last-minute emotional reaction ... there must be more to our worship of God than just an emotional response ... it must also include repentance! God wants to be more than just a God of a crisis moment.

It is tragic that these men and women did not repent of their sins, even after witnessing God's power to raise the dead and transport them to heaven! Miracles alone will not convince anyone to accept Christ ... there must be conviction in the heart that one is a sinner and in need of a savior before transformation can take place. Think of the many Pharisees and others who saw Jesus perform miracles and still did not believe ... faith is not always born from miracles. It is born from the Word of God. "Faith comes by hearing, and hearing by the Word of God" (Rom. 10:17 - KJV).

For 3½ years, these people heard the truth from God's witnesses, they observed God's supernatural power to protect these witnesses, they saw God's power by miracles done by their command ... such things as plagues and the heavens shut up with no rain ... and finally they see God raise two dead men who had been dead for over three days and translate them to heaven ... and still they don't believe! What does it take to believe? Do you only glorify God but fail to yield your life to Him? Is God real in your life?

Despite all these things, there is still more coming ... without positive results, yet! This is only the end of the second woe ... the third is about to strike. There is every indication that those who have already hardened their hearts will not change even after another round of God's prodding.

Seven years of the Antichrist's rule have not yet caused sinners to turn to God. What a sad reality!

The good news, however, is this: Though Satan and his servants have tried for seven years to destroy God's plans and take over the planet, they are about to be finished! The Antichrist and Satan have not been able to destroy God's Word or the light of the Gospel!

Satan will fail ... so why follow a failure!?

The final woe will come quickly since this is now already at the end of the seven years of tribulation ... it will be the third and final woe, and God will usher in an age of righteousness. Why not be part of God's plan instead of Satan's? Do you hear His call on your life? Are you a witness for Christ?

God's calling on His servants never changes ... preach the Gospel to every creature! Even when the world becomes darkest, God will raise up witnesses to the Gospel of Jesus Christ. Only after they had finished the task did God call these two witnesses home.

Today, you have a choice, the Gospel or your sins. Choose well!

The Conqueror

Revelation 11:15-12:17

Then the seventh angel blew his trumpet, and there were loud voices in heaven, saying, "The kingdom of the world has become the kingdom of our Lord and of his Christ, and he shall reign forever and ever." And the twenty-four elders who sit on their thrones before God fell on their faces and worshiped God, saying,

"We give thanks to you, Lord God Almighty, who is and who was, for you have taken your great power and begun to reign. The nations raged, but your wrath came, and the time for the dead to be judged, and for rewarding your servants, the prophets and saints, and those who fear your name, both small and great, and for destroying the destroyers of the earth."

Then God's temple in heaven was opened, and the

ark of his covenant was seen within his temple. There were flashes of lightning, rumblings, peals of thunder, an earthquake, and heavy hail.

And a great sign appeared in heaven: a woman clothed with the sun, with the moon under her feet, and on her head a crown of twelve stars. She was pregnant and was crying out in birth pains and the agony of giving birth. And another sign appeared in heaven: behold, a great red dragon, with seven heads and ten horns, and on his heads seven diadems. His tail swept down a third of the stars of heaven and cast them to the earth. And the dragon stood before the woman who was about to give birth, so that when she bore her child he might devour it. She gave birth to a male child, one who is to rule all the nations with a rod of iron, but her child was caught up to God and to his throne, and the woman fled into the wilderness, where she has a place prepared by God, in which she is to be nourished for 1,260 days.

Now war arose in heaven, Michael and his angels fighting against the dragon. And the dragon and his angels fought back, but he was defeated, and there was no longer any place for them in heaven. And the great dragon was thrown down, that ancient serpent, who is called the devil and Satan, the deceiver of the whole world—he was thrown down to the earth, and his angels were thrown down with him. And I heard a loud voice in heaven, saying, "Now the salvation and the power and the kingdom of our God and the authority of his Christ have come, for the accuser of our brothers has been thrown down, who accuses them day and night before our God. And they have conquered him by the blood of the Lamb and by the word of their testimony, for they loved not their lives even unto death. Therefore, rejoice, O heavens and you who dwell in them! But woe to you, O earth and sea, for the devil has come down to you in great wrath, because he knows that his time is short!"

And when the dragon saw that he had been thrown down to the earth, he pursued the woman who had given birth to the male child. But the woman was given the two wings of the great eagle so that she might fly from the serpent into the wilderness, to the place where she is to be nourished for a time, and times, and half a time. The serpent poured water like a river out of his mouth after the woman, to sweep her away with a flood. But the earth came to the help of the woman, and the earth opened its mouth and swallowed the river that the dragon had poured from his mouth. Then the dragon became furious with the woman and went off to make war on the rest of her offspring, on those who keep the commandments of God and hold to the testimony of Jesus. And he stood on the sand of the sea.

Mankind's history is full of the struggle between good and evil. Our actual history reflects this. Our literature reflects this as does our films ... our stories are almost always about the struggle between the two.

Think about some of the biggest hit movies ... what do they all have in common? Most of them present an evil power or person making inroads in conquering the world as we know it, then along comes someone who rallies a challenge against this evil and, ultimately, good is triumphant.

There is something in the human heart that both fears evil and hopes for good to overcome it. This situation is real and NOT JUST A STORY!

The story of Jesus is the fulfillment of all of man's hopes. Satan and evil are real ... and Jesus' life and power are the forces that will deal Satan his final defeat. Even when it looks like Satan has won the day, we must remember that he is already a defeated foe!

Satan as the serpent in the garden of Eden threatened God's plans for man, but God found a way to destroy Satan ... and with his final defeat Christ will rule as conqueror over the earth.

The Bible clearly teaches that Christ has vanquished Satan's power and will one day even vanquish his presence from the earth. For you to be victorious, you must belong to Christ.

When the seventh seal was opened, "there was silence in heaven for about half an hour" (Rev. 8:1). However, as the seventh trumpet sounds, there are "loud voices in heaven." Quite a contrast! Why? Here Christ is revealed as the conqueror ... hardly a reason to be silent!

We are witnessing here the final events of the tribulation period, the last 3½ years. It will be a horrible time of evil. Satan will lash out as never before ... but he does not win! There is little question about the final outcome, as already those in heaven are proclaiming Christ's triumph. Without even finishing the events of the tribulation period, the proclamation in heaven is that Jesus is about to rule and reign forever! Never has there been doubt in heaven who the victor over sin is!

The day Christ arose from the dead, Satan's power ended ... the snake who had bruised the heel of mankind now has his head crushed as promised by God in Genesis 3:15. Even in Jesus' time on earth (before the cross) the demons of hell had to obey Him ... it is tragic that any human being would so ignore

Christ who alone has power over evil! All that is left to Satan in fury! The power of Christ is so great that even Satan's evil is turned to accomplishing God's purposes! If Satan is the biggest loser in the universe, what does that make all those who will follow him instead of Christ?

The temple in heaven is now opened, and the mention of the ark of His covenant reminds the reader that God's promises and power have not been forgotten or lost ... they are symbols of God's covenant to destroy evil and save Israel.

The "woman clothed with the sun, with the moon under her feet and a crown of twelve stars" is most likely a reference to Israel. God has a plan ... for which Abraham was raised up to be the father of a nation in which the Messiah would be born. God's plan was from the beginning of time. God was always aware of Satan's schemes to destroy.

Even as this "woman" was about to give birth to a son, a son who would "rule the nations with an iron scepter" (12:5), the dragon stood in front of her with the hopes of "devouring her child." Clearly, Satan attempted to destroy Christ when He was born. This was evident by the decree given to kill all the male children around Bethlehem who were two years old and younger. Satan also attempted to destroy Christ on the cross of Calvary. Perhaps at first Satan thought he had won the victory on the cross, but was he sorely mistaken ... which is always the case with him!

So many times throughout history ... and at the end of time ... it appears that evil has won, that good has been vanquished, but the truth is that evil will NOT prevail!

Satan is full of hatred, envy, pride, lies ... he cannot accept the consequences of his own actions, and he foolishly commits himself to try and destroy God and God's people! It is a tragic picture ... but God not only protects the child born (Christ) and snatches Him up to heaven (the Ascension of Christ) ... He also protects the woman (Israel). Note that God protects the woman an equal period of time that Satan is chasing her (1,260 days as mentioned here — 3½ years). The point is simply that God protects His own for as long as Satan does his evil deeds. God's people are never unprotected! Satan has so often tried to destroy Israel ... he is fixated on destroying all things that God blesses.

Here at the end of time, Satan wages war in heaven as well as on earth ... but Michael the arch-angel fights back successfully. Michael is an archangel apparently chosen to protect Israel throughout time ... in Daniel 12:1 he is also mentioned as a protector for Israel. As God prepares to usher in the millennial reign of Christ, Satan is cast out of heaven for good!

Satan failed miserably in destroying Christ ... and he will fail ultimately in destroying Israel ... and Christ will rule and reign forever!

Again, we hear the "loud voice in heaven" proclaiming Christ's victory! Satan's war against God is coming to a close ... he won't be allowed to make accusations against God's people anymore! We know from the book of Job that Satan at times comes before God in heaven to accuse the believers ... but this freedom is about to be lost forever. No longer will Satan be able to accuse the brethren, for he is banished from heaven for good!

Satan has gained nothing ... he only revealed God's great grace and power instead of destroying it.

Note that all those who overcame Satan did so in the same way: "by the blood of the lamb and by the word of their testimony..." Our power over Satan does not arise from within us ... that is why all sinners will fail to overcome Satan! The ability to overcome Satan starts at the cross and follows through by our testimony. Once we accept Christ and His sacrifice, we are out of reach by Satan's powers ... for we have been delivered, and only then can we live a godly life.

Do you want to live outside of Satan's control and

power over your life? To do so will require you to accept the life of the only one who has beaten the devil and death ... Jesus Christ. No other religion has conquered death! No other religion has an empty grave for its founder! No other religion has a founder who has completely defeated evil. All other religions require you to find your way to God. Only in Christ do we see a God who found His way to us by becoming one of us and dying for us. Do you still want to stand against the devil alone and without God?

You can imagine that Satan's expulsion from heaven and his imminent final defeat does not sit well with him. He becomes enraged even more ... and he pursues the "woman who had given birth to the male child." This means Satan's final crazed act will be a final attempt to destroy Israel! As Satan has tried before, he will try again to destroy the chosen people, and once more God will provide a miracle of help for Israel!

Israel will be given "two wings of a great eagle, so that she might fly to the place prepared for her in the desert, where she would be taken care of for a time, times and half a time, out of the serpent's reach." God will protect them again supernaturally during these 3½ years — the meaning of the phrase "for a time, times and half a time." Satan's powers are always contained. The only power in the universe that can protect against Satan is the God of Abraham, Isaac, and Jacob Himself!

Such protection will only cause Satan to spew out a flood of evil to sweep Israel away — Revelation 12:15 in the NIV tells us: "Then from his mouth the serpent spewed water like a river, to overtake the woman and sweep her away with the torrent." However, God opens up the earth to swallow this flood and Israel is saved again! Revelation 12:16 in the NIV goes on to say: "But the earth helped the woman by opening its mouth and swallowing the river that the dragon had spewed out of his mouth." Every attempt of Satan to destroy God's plan and people will fail! This was seen when Rome tried to destroy Israel. This was seen when Hitler tried to destroy the Jews.

This final loss by Satan will send him into a rage that will include attacking not only Israel, but all believers. Revelation 12:17 in the NIV finishes up with: "Then the dragon was enraged at the woman and went off to make war against the rest of her offspring — those who obey God's commandments and hold to the testimony of Jesus." Nothing Satan can do will shake God's plan or destroy God's people. There is no safer place to be than in the arms of God!

If God can protect His own when Satan is at his worst, how much more can He help us today? Christ IS THE CONQUEROR ... and Satan is the conquered! Have you accepted Christ into your life, or are you outside the protection of God? You either belong to God or to Satan ... the choice is yours!

Why stick with a loser? Satan has no hope of victory, and all he brings to his followers is painful loss. Satan's ONLY desire for you is your destruction, and God's only desire for you is reconstruction!

There have been plenty of times in history when things were so bleak as to defy the notion that good triumphs over evil! So often it seems that evil wins and good loses. Yet, today good still survives ... despite those evil times, and we must remember that no matter how dark our trial, we will overcome BY THE BLOOD OF THE LAMB, not our own strength. Christ is victor ... and all those who follow Him are victors through Him!

Romans 8:37 in the NIV encourages us with these words: "No, in all these things we are more than conquerors through him who loved us." Follow the true conqueror!

The Choice

Revelation 13:1-18

And I saw a beast rising out of the sea, with ten horns and seven heads, with ten diadems on its horns and blasphemous names on its heads. And the beast that I saw was like a leopard; its feet were like a bear's, and its mouth was like a lion's mouth. And to it the dragon gave his power and his throne and great authority. One of its heads seemed to have a mortal wound, but its mortal wound was healed, and the whole earth marveled as they followed the beast. And they worshiped the dragon, for he had given his authority to the beast, and they worshiped the beast, saying, "Who is like the beast, and who can fight against it?"

And the beast was given a mouth uttering haughty and blasphemous words, and it was allowed to exercise authority for forty-two months. It opened

189

its mouth to utter blasphemies against God, blaspheming his name and his dwelling, that is, those who dwell in heaven. Also it was allowed to make war on the saints and to conquer them. And authority was given it over every tribe and people and language and nation, and all who dwell on earth will worship it, everyone whose name has not been written before the foundation of the world in the book of life of the Lamb who was slain. If anyone has an ear, let him hear:

If anyone is to be taken captive, to captivity he goes; if anyone is to be slain with the sword, with the sword must he be slain.

Here is a call for the endurance and faith of the saints.

Then I saw another beast rising out of the earth. It had two horns like a lamb and it spoke like a dragon. It exercises all the authority of the first beast in its presence, and makes the earth and its inhabitants worship the first beast, whose mortal wound was healed. It performs great signs, even making fire come down from heaven to earth in front of people, and by the signs that it is allowed to work in the presence of the beast it deceives those who dwell on earth, telling them to make an image for the beast that was wounded by the sword and yet lived. And it was allowed to give breath to the image of the beast, so that the image of the beast might even speak and might cause those who would not worship the image of the beast to be slain. Also it causes all, both small and great, both rich and poor, both free and slave, to be marked on the right hand or the forehead, so that no one can buy or sell unless he has the mark, that is, the name of the beast or the number of its name. This calls for wisdom: let the one who has understanding calculate the number of the beast, for it is the number of a man, and his number is 666.

This chapter in Revelation is widely known. Hollywood has made movies about this chapter in the Bible, although seldom containing the truth of the Bible ... there has been graffiti painted all over the world with the number 666, it has been spoken about since the time of the disciples, and it has struck fear into the hearts of mankind for thousands of years.

Everyone fears the number 666 ... it is the symbol of evil everywhere!

While we are fascinated about the "mark of the beast," we must not forget that the power of evil that will one day express itself through the Antichrist is already present in the world, and we should be concerned about the power of evil in our OWN heart! 1 John 2:18 in the NIV says: "Dear children, this is the last hour; and as you have heard that the antichrist is coming, even now many antichrists have come. This is how we know it is the last hour."

With the seeds of the Antichrist already in the world and men's hearts today, no wonder it will be POSSIBLE for the Antichrist to find a following!

Some people have said that they don't believe in all this stuff about the devil and a future Antichrist ... but the Bible clearly teaches that both today and tomorrow offers a choice for all human beings, the choice between God and the devil. There is no middle ground. We are followers of Christ or the Antichrist. The "beast coming out of the sea" is the Antichrist. The sea in antiquity often represented humanity and evil. The metaphor of the "sea of humanity" expresses this. It also represented a mysteriously frightening place. In antiquity they thought you would fall off the planet if you traveled too far out to sea, so it was associated with evil and fear. The image here is that the Antichrist will be an evil human who arises from the human race but is energized by Satan.

The ten horns with ten crowns represent authority and power. The seven heads represent ruling power. This picture is nearly identical to the dragon mentioned in 12:3: "an enormous red dragon with seven heads and ten horns and seven crowns on his heads." It clearly establishes that this "beast" or Antichrist is closely connected to the "dragon" which is called "Satan" in 12:9.

Satan is going to offer the world a false god ... a false trinity! Satan will be like the "father." This human being energized by Satan will be the "Antichrist." Later in this chapter, another "beast" arises from the earth which will give breath to the idol of the Antichrist, giving breath like a "spirit" ... albeit an "unholy spirit."

Satan's desire, unlike God's, is to destroy man, not save us. Some people find it hard to believe that this could be real ... but everything else in the Bible has been, and so will this! Satan's desires and goals are obvious ... to conquer the saints, to blaspheme God, and to promote himself! How different from Jesus Christ is this Antichrist! Jesus conquered sin, not sinners ... He honored God, not blasphemed Him, and He sacrificed Himself for lost man, He didn't sacrifice man. Why anyone chooses to ignore the real Christ is a mystery!!!

Nearly all the world will worship this false messiah when he comes. Look at how men follow evil today. This is not a far-fetched idea! Today we tend to think of Satan and evil power as being in the form of witches and pentagrams ... these are easy to avoid and we recoil at the idea of accepting those things ... BUT, this isn't the essence of evil. True evil is far more sinister and subtle, but so powerful! ... Real evil is found in the hearts of selfish humanity who seek to make others serve their own ends ... this is the essence of evil and sin. This is why evil catches us off guard. It doesn't appear so evil until we finally see its bitter fruit.

It requires a firm commitment to live for God ... anyone can be evil. It follows the path of least resistance! It seems so often that evil wins the day ... but we must not cave in. Evil's day will end. God is at work even when it doesn't appear that way! Notice that John encourages those who will undergo terrible times as saints to be patient and faithful to the end! It requires a firm commitment on the part of the saints, for it will appear that they cannot win ... but Christ IS IN CONTROL. Note that the passage states that the Antichrist will only rule for 42 months ... it is a limited period. It will end!

Only those whose names are written in the Lamb's book of life will not be overtaken by this Antichrist. Is your name in this book? It is a choice you must make!

To fool the world into worshipping him, the

Antichrist will experience a fatal wound ... and be resurrected ... causing the world to marvel at him! This will be a counterfeit resurrection! Satan never does anything unique. He copies God but for his own ends!

To copy God even more, another beast arrives on the scene, one that comes out of the earth ... this is the "false prophet" who speaks and breathes Satan's powers ... like an unholy spirit, a counterfeit of God's Holy Spirit. This false prophet will do great miracles like causing fire to fall from heaven like Elijah in the full view of humanity! This false prophet will energize the idol of the Antichrist so that it can speak ... and cause mankind to worship the beast!

How is it that evil will flourish so easily? It meshes well with our selfish sinful hearts.

Satan is too smart to entice us to follow him by showing us evil directly. He traps us with his miraculous signs that look an awful lot like God's wonderful miracles! The difference, however, is great. God does miracles to liberate us with His love. Satan does miracles to entrap us into worshipping him, to imprison us for destruction, and to encourage us to hate. As we move away from God, we move closer to Satan, and the world will (and is continuing to) move closer and closer to Satan's evil.

We do not have to yield to Satan's devices and plans. Jesus Christ has made a way of escape from both sin and the power of sin. Satan will push humanity into making a choice, between him and God! In a very real way, this is already here! In our life, we are either following God or the devil. There is no middle ground. A choice must be made! Satan always tries to make man believe that God is not a good choice!

Ultimately, the choice will be forced one way or another. In the future, it will involve taking the mark of the beast. Today, though, it is just as real a choice as it will be in the future. We can no more ignore this choice today than we will be able to ignore it in the future! The fact is that Satan is setting the groundwork today for his evil reign, and so often we fail to see it or take it seriously!

Satan's mark is interesting ... 666. We don't really know what this means, and perhaps we are not supposed to know. Maybe it will only be clear at the time it needs to be clear. But John does say this is the "number of man" — not "a man." Maybe it is a reference to the fact that the best Satan can offer is an unholy trinity whose members each fall short of perfection, with each of the three sixes being one less than the perfect number seven. And since there are three sixes ... one number for each member of his counterfeit trinity ... it seems that Satan falls short once more. It is interesting to note that the numerical value of Jesus' name is 888, one number ABOVE perfection for each member of the trinity!

Satan will fall short ... and how tragic that so many will seal their fate with him .... But MANY people have sealed their fate with him TODAY! While they may not wear a physical mark, their hearts are turned away from God, and they have Satan's stamp in them now! It is not just a future decision that people will need to make. We all, in our lifetime, are called upon to make this choice.

It is also interesting that this "mark of the beast" is put either on the forehead or the RIGHT hand ... the Jews put portions of the Scriptures on their forehead or LEFT hands in small boxes called phylacteries. Satan appears to be counterfeiting this, too! The phylacteries represented their acceptance of the covenant and their being bound by God's covenant. The "mark of the beast" represents being bound to Satan. To take this mark is to seal your fate!

Satan is slowly edging the world toward his destructive plans, but God will be the final victor! There is a clear choice to make ... you WILL serve one or the other! Today is the day of choice. Choose Christ and not Antichrist!

One day every person will have one final choice to make between God and Satan ... but in a very real way that choices faces us each day! We stand amazed to think people will choose the mark of the beast, but if we aren't actively choosing to follow Christ, we are no better off today!

Will you choose Jesus Christ or Antichrist? What choice are you making NOW!?

The Climax

Revelation 14:1-15:8

Then I looked, and behold, on Mount Zion stood the Lamb, and with him 144,000 who had his name and his Father's name written on their foreheads. And I heard a voice from heaven like the roar of many waters and like the sound of loud thunder. The voice I heard was like the sound of harpists playing on their harps, and they were singing a new song before the throne and before the four living creatures and before the elders. No one could learn that song except the 144,000 who had been redeemed from the earth. It is these who have not defiled themselves with women, for they are virgins. It is these who follow the Lamb wherever he goes. These have been redeemed from mankind as firstfruits for God and the Lamb, and in their mouth no lie was found, for they are blameless.

Then I saw another angel flying directly overhead, with an eternal gospel to proclaim to those who dwell on earth, to every nation and tribe and language and people. And he said with a loud voice, "Fear God and give him glory, because the hour of his judgment has come, and worship him who made heaven and earth, the sea and the springs of water."

Another angel, a second, followed, saying, "Fallen, fallen is Babylon the great, she who made all nations drink the wine of the passion of her sexual immorality."

And another angel, a third, followed them, saying with a loud voice, "If anyone worships the beast and its image and receives a mark on his forehead or on his hand, he also will drink the wine of God's wrath, poured full strength into the cup of his anger, and he will be tormented with fire and sulfur in the presence of the holy angels and in the presence of the Lamb. And the smoke of their torment goes up forever and ever, and they have no rest, day or night, these worshipers of the beast and its image, and whoever receives the mark of its name."

Here is a call for the endurance of the saints, those who keep the commandments of God and their faith in Jesus.

And I heard a voice from heaven saying, "Write this: Blessed are the dead who die in the Lord from now on." "Blessed indeed," says the Spirit, "that they may rest from their labors, for their deeds follow them!"

Then I looked, and behold, a white cloud, and seated on the cloud one like a son of man, with a golden crown on his head, and a sharp sickle in his hand. And another angel came out of the temple, calling with a loud voice to him who sat on the cloud, "Put in your sickle, and reap, for the hour to reap has come, for the harvest of the earth is fully ripe." So he who sat on the cloud swung his sickle across the earth, and the earth was reaped.

Then another angel came out of the temple in heaven, and he too had a sharp sickle. And another angel came out from the altar, the angel who has authority over the fire, and he called with a loud voice to the one who had the sharp sickle, "Put in your sickle and gather the clusters from the vine of the earth, for its grapes are ripe." So the angel swung his sickle across the earth and gathered the grape harvest of the earth and threw it into the great winepress of the wrath of God. And the winepress was trodden outside the city, and blood flowed from the winepress, as high as a horse's bridle, for 1,600 stadia.

Then I saw another sign in heaven, great and amazing, seven angels with seven plagues, which are the last, for with them the wrath of God is finished.

And I saw what appeared to be a sea of glass mingled with fire—and also those who had conquered the beast and its image and the number of its name, standing beside the sea of glass with harps of God in their hands. And they sing the song of Moses, the servant of God, and the song of the Lamb, saying,

"Great and amazing are your deeds, O Lord God the Almighty! Just and true are your ways, O King of the nations! Who will not fear, O Lord, and glorify your name? For you alone are holy. All nations will come and worship you, for your righteous acts have been revealed."

After this I looked, and the sanctuary of the tent of witness in heaven was opened, and out of the sanctuary came the seven angels with the seven plagues, clothed in pure, bright linen, with golden sashes around their chests. And one of the four living creatures gave to the seven angels seven golden bowls full of the wrath of God who lives forever and ever, and the sanctuary was filled with smoke from the glory of God and from his power, and no one could enter the sanctuary until the

When most people think about the future, it usually doesn't include eternity! Most of our life, we are looking forward to a future that involves only the things of this life. Even as we age, we are only thinking about the future in terms of retirement and not beyond that. Yet, when death comes, we won't be thinking about the things of this world. What will occupy our mind then is the real future, eternity.

It's reported that at the end of Thomas Edison's successful life, he roused out of a coma long enough to say, "It is very beautiful over there," before breathing his last. Even Thomas Edison at the end wasn't thinking about his inventions and earthly accomplishments. His final words were about eternity!

Isn't it amazing that we spend so little time thinking about THAT future? So many of us go to great lengths to plan for a trip somewhere, making careful calculations, getting things in order before we leave ... but yet we FAIL to plan for the greatest trip we will ever make, the journey after death.

Eternity is stamped on humanity ... only, in our fast-paced secular world, we have put eternity out of our mind. Shouldn't we take seriously the eternal future we all will face and properly prepare for it? The Bible clearly teaches that one of two destinies is in the future for every living person, and the experience we have tomorrow is based on the experience we have today. Today in Christ ... tomorrow in heaven; today without Christ ... tomorrow in hell.

John's emphasis in the closing chapters of Revelation are about the certainty of everlasting life ... and where we will spend it. The righteous will receive their rewards. The unrighteous will experience God's wrath.

John is making an obvious contrast here of those who have been "marked by God with His name on their foreheads" and those "marked by the beast on their foreheads." We belong to God or the devil. Such ownership will determine where we spend eternity.

The chapter opens with the "pure, the blameless" ... those who have embraced Christ as their Lord. They have not compromised with this world. They have lived by God's standards rather than this world's or their own. God's people should stand out as a holy people in a world of darkness! If we were judged today by our lifestyles, would there be enough evidence to convict us of being a Christian? John says that these believers are not only "pure and blameless," but that "they follow the lamb wherever He goes." Can this be said about you? This group of 144,000 that are here in heaven is probably the same group mentioned in Revelation 7:4 ... they have been martyred for their faith, and they died without compromise, proving that it is possible to live an uncompromising life. Heaven is the reward and joy for all those who follow Christ in this life.

The "hour of judgment has come." John says there will be a time of judgment for how we live. While sin seems to go unpunished now, this will not always be the case. There will be a day when God will fully deal with sin. The only reason we don't see this yet is that God is gracious and is still giving time for people to repent of their sins. This future judgment can be avoided ... IF WE PLAN wisely NOW!

The future always depends on what we do today, even in the natural! If you don't put money aside for retirement, you will be at the mercy of the state. If you don't invest today, you will have no dividends tomorrow ... and if you don't attend to spiritual issues today, tomorrow could be too late! The great powers and nations of this world will one day all fall ... this has always been true in history, and the future will show this to be true, also. The only kingdom that will continue to stand in the future is the kingdom of God!

The future destination for each human being is a permanent one. Once in heaven, always in heaven ... and once in hell, always in hell! With so much at stake for your future, can you really afford to ignore preparing for it today?

As certain as the rewards of the righteous are, so is the certainty of judgment on the unrighteous. John clearly reveals that a day is coming when God will bring in the final harvest ... every farmer knows that there is a harvest day when he plants his fields. Because sinners now don't see God's final judgments, they assume that this will never come. Accountability is a principle of life ... in every area.

While our world likes to ignore the possibilities of eternal punishment, it does not mean that it doesn't exist. Far more people believe in heaven than believe in hell ... how convenient! Most people believe that if there is a heaven, they will go to it, and very few who admit there could be a hell believe they will go there. The moment of death could be a real eye opener!

The tragic reality is that all those who experience God's wrath could have avoided it. Christ made a way of escape, but we must accept it. Too often we refuse to accept God's ways, and we insist on living by our own standards ... real freedom can only be found in Christ, and today is the opportunity for accepting Him.

The great contrast is shown in this chapter. The righteous sing a new song, a song only the redeemed can possibly know. The unrighteous experience God's wrath with no hope ... their future is a godless one. The final judgment on sin will begin ... there is coming a day when sin will no longer go unpunished. It will be judged.

All the cynics today who reject God will one day face the reality of God whether they believe it now or not ... so often the world foolishly ignores the reality of God, and they choose not to see Him.

These final judgments from God are different from earlier ones. The earlier ones gave opportunity for change, while these contain nothing redemptive. They are simply the final price tag for rebellion against God.

The finality is horrible, and completely avoidable NOW ... what will the climax to your life be like? Do you know what your future holds? Will you be playing a harp or harping against God? If you are willing to make elaborate plans for an earthly trip, why not make adequate plans for your eternal trip?

So often it has appeared that evil has won the day ... but the cry for true justice has not gone unheard. The day will come when the rule of evil will end. Evil WILL be punished, and righteousness WILL be rewarded. We do not live for God in vain. We will see the day when sin is defeated, and we can celebrate the victory over sin.

Are you ready for THAT day?

The Cataclysm

Revelation 16:1-18:24

Then I heard a loud voice from the temple telling the seven angels, "Go and pour out on the earth the seven bowls of the wrath of God."

So the first angel went and poured out his bowl on the earth, and harmful and painful sores came upon the people who bore the mark of the beast and worshiped its image.

The second angel poured out his bowl into the sea, and it became like the blood of a corpse, and every living thing died that was in the sea.

The third angel poured out his bowl into the rivers and the springs of water, and they became blood. And I heard the angel in charge of the waters say,

"Just are you, O Holy One, who is and who was, for you brought these judgments. For they have shed

209

the blood of saints and prophets, and you have given them blood to drink. It is what they deserve!"

And I heard the altar saying, "Yes, Lord God the Almighty, true and just are your judgments!"

The fourth angel poured out his bowl on the sun, and it was allowed to scorch people with fire. They were scorched by the fierce heat, and they cursed the name of God who had power over these plagues. They did not repent and give him glory.

The fifth angel poured out his bowl on the throne of the beast, and its kingdom was plunged into darkness. People gnawed their tongues in anguish and cursed the God of heaven for their pain and sores. They did not repent of their deeds.

The sixth angel poured out his bowl on the great river Euphrates, and its water was dried up, to prepare the way for the kings from the east. And I saw, coming out of the mouth of the dragon and out of the mouth of the beast and out of the mouth of the false prophet, three unclean spirits like frogs. For they are demonic spirits, performing signs, who go abroad to the kings of the whole world, to assemble them for battle on the great day of God the Almighty. ("Behold, I am coming like a thief! Blessed is the one who stays awake, keeping his garments on, that he may not go about naked and be seen exposed!") And they assembled them at *the place that in Hebrew is called Armageddon.*

The seventh angel poured out his bowl into the air, and a loud voice came out of the temple, from the throne, saying, "It is done!" And there were flashes of lightning, rumblings, peals of thunder, and a great earthquake such as there had never been since man was on the earth, so great was that earthquake. The great city was split into three parts, and the cities of the nations fell, and God remembered Babylon the great, to make her drain the cup of the wine of the fury of his wrath. And every island fled away, and no mountains were to be found. And great hailstones, about one hundred pounds each, fell from heaven on people; and they cursed God for the plague of the hail, because the plague was so severe.

Then one of the seven angels who had the seven bowls came and said to me, "Come, I will show you the judgment of the great prostitute who is seated on many waters, with whom the kings of the earth have committed sexual immorality, and with the wine of whose sexual immorality the dwellers on earth have become drunk." And he carried me away in the Spirit into a wilderness, and I saw a woman sitting on a scarlet beast that was full of blasphemous names, and it had seven heads and ten horns. The woman was arrayed in purple and scarlet, and adorned with gold and jewels and pearls, holding in her hand a golden cup full of abominations and the impurities of her sexual immorality. And on her forehead was written a name of mystery: "Babylon the great, mother of prostitutes and of earth's abominations." And I saw the woman, drunk with the blood of the saints, the blood of the martyrs of Jesus.

When I saw her, I marveled greatly. But the angel said to me, "Why do you marvel? I will tell you the mystery of the woman, and of the beast with seven heads and ten horns that carries her. The beast that you saw was, and is not, and is about to rise from the bottomless pit and go to destruction. And the dwellers on earth whose names have not been written in the book of life from the foundation of the world will marvel to see the beast, because it was and is not and is to come. This calls for a mind with wisdom: the seven heads are seven mountains on which the woman is seated; they are also seven kings, five of whom have fallen, one is, the other has not yet come, and when he does come he must remain only a little while. As for the beast that was and is not, it is an eighth but it belongs to the seven, and it goes to destruction. And the ten horns that you saw are ten kings who have not yet received royal power, but they are to receive authority as kings for one hour, together with the beast. These are of one mind, and they hand over their power and authority to the beast. They will make war on the Lamb, and the Lamb will conquer them, for he is Lord of lords and King of kings, and those with him are called and chosen and faithful."

And the angel said to me, "The waters that you saw, where the prostitute is seated, are peoples and multitudes and nations and languages. And the ten horns that you saw, they and the beast will hate the prostitute. They will make her desolate and naked, and devour her flesh and burn her up with fire, for God has put it into their hearts to carry out his purpose by being of one mind and handing over their royal power to the beast, until the words of God are fulfilled. And the woman that you saw is the great city that has dominion over the kings of the earth."

After this I saw another angel coming down from heaven, having great authority, and the earth was made bright with his glory. And he called out with a mighty voice,

"Fallen, fallen is Babylon the great! She has become a dwelling place for demons, a haunt for every unclean spirit, a haunt for every unclean bird, a haunt for every unclean and detestable beast. For all nations have drunk the wine of the passion of her sexual immorality, and the kings of the earth have committed immorality with her, and the

merchants of the earth have grown rich from the power of her luxurious living."

Then I heard another voice from heaven saying, "Come out of her, my people, lest you take part in her sins, lest you share in her plagues; for her sins are heaped high as heaven, and God has remembered her iniquities. Pay her back as she herself has paid back others, and repay her double for her deeds; mix a double portion for her in the cup she mixed. As she glorified herself and lived in luxury, so give her a like measure of torment and mourning, since in her heart she says, 'I sit as a queen, I am no widow, and mourning I shall never see.' For this reason her plagues will come in a single day, death and mourning and famine, and she will be burned up with fire; for mighty is the Lord God who has judged her."

And the kings of the earth, who committed sexual immorality and lived in luxury with her, will weep and wail over her when they see the smoke of her burning. They will stand far off, in fear of her torment, and say, "Alas! Alas! You great city, you mighty city, Babylon! For in a single hour your judgment has come."

And the merchants of the earth weep and mourn for her, since no one buys their cargo anymore, cargo of gold, silver, jewels, pearls, fine linen, *purple cloth, silk, scarlet cloth, all kinds of scented wood, all kinds of articles of ivory, all kinds of articles of costly wood, bronze, iron and marble, cinnamon, spice, incense, myrrh, frankincense, wine, oil, fine flour, wheat, cattle and sheep, horses and chariots, and slaves, that is, human souls.*

"The fruit for which your soul longed has gone from you, and all your delicacies and your splendors are lost to you, never to be found again!"

The merchants of these wares, who gained wealth from her, will stand far off, in fear of her torment, weeping and mourning aloud,

"Alas, alas, for the great city that was clothed in fine linen, in purple and scarlet, adorned with gold, with jewels, and with pearls! For in a single hour all this wealth has been laid waste."

And all shipmasters and seafaring men, sailors and all whose trade is on the sea, stood far off and cried out as they saw the smoke of her burning, "What city was like the great city?"

And they threw dust on their heads as they wept and mourned, crying out, "Alas, alas, for the great city where all who had ships at sea grew rich by her wealth! For in a single hour she has been laid waste. Rejoice over her, O heaven, and you saints and apostles and prophets, for God has given judgment for you against her!"

Then a mighty angel took up a stone like a great millstone and threw it into the sea, saying, "So will Babylon the great city be thrown down with violence, and will be found no more; and the sound of harpists and musicians, of flute players and trumpeters, will be heard in you no more, and a craftsman of any craft will be found in you no more, and the sound of the mill will be heard in you no more, and the light of a lamp will shine in you no more, and the voice of bridegroom and bride will be heard in you no more, for your merchants were the great ones of the earth, and all nations were deceived by your sorcery. And in her was found the blood of prophets and of saints, and of all who have been slain on earth."

The history of evil is a long and terrible one. One does not have to go back too far in history to witness the terrible price tag of evil on the human race. Evil does not come from animals or technology; it comes from the sinful heart.

Unfortunately, the days of evil are not over, and in fact they will be with us until the end of time. Though we become more sophisticated technologically, though our wealth continues to grow ... evil is also spreading its influence. We are living in times when it is NOT just the religious people saying we need a spiritual renewal. Even TV producer Norman Lear and director Oliver Stone are recorded as saying that we are becoming decadent and in need of a spiritual revival.

There has been a gradual numbing in our culture toward evil, a process seen in history just before an onslaught of horrible deeds. Indeed, no one becomes suddenly evil overnight. It is usually a gradual process.

So often it appears that evil flourishes and escapes punishment while good so often goes unrewarded ... but this will not always be the case. Indeed, God is very much concerned about evil in this world, and it will one day be dealt with completely, so don't lose hope or encouragement. God is in control!

John describes the final set of seven judgments during the tribulation. These final judgment bowls will fully touch the world, not partially as earlier ones appeared to do. Evil will not escape punishment. God's justice will be complete and fair.

This is why as Christians we don't lose heart NOW when we see evil flourish without punishment ... we know that God will balance the scales in time. If this were not so, it would be a maddening thing to see that evil has so often gotten away with so many atrocities

... but we know that this won't continue to be true. This is what keeps us plugging away doing good; we know that our labors WON'T be in vain.

So often the world worries about the wrong stuff ... for many years we worried about new and greater weapons ... and while this is surely a concern, the real issue should be the heart of men who would use them!

John's vision clearly shows a time when God will completely deal with evil ... when sin and evil will truly be punished fairly! You can escape human justice ... but not heavenly justice! Nothing escapes God's notice.

IRONICALLY, when God punishes evil and evil doers, they DO NOT REPENT! Notice in Revelation 16:9, 11, 21 — the wicked REFUSE to repent and they continue to curse God! The hardness of the human heart can be remarkable!

In the midst of evil's punishment, God encourages faithfulness! Notice that John states that Jesus Christ is "COMING LIKE A THIEF." It will be swift and unexpected by the wicked. Christ will not allow evil to rule this planet forever.

No one anticipates the coming of a thief. If they did, they would be ready for them! Will you be ready when Christ comes? His coming is only like a thief to those NOT ready! Notice Jesus' words here: "Blessed is he who stays awake (alert) and keeps his clothes with him, so that he may not go naked and be shamefully exposed." The clothes of the believer are the robes of Christ's righteousness. Don't ever take them off! To be found naked would be a shame ... and a terrible loss.

We don't have to be alarmed at evil ... concerned, yes, alarmed, no ... because we know the final score! Satan is no match for God! We need to do all we can to thwart evil, and we don't have to be overcome by its existence. We are certain of two things: Evil will increase as the end of time approaches, and God will win and overcome all evil ... we win!

John now reveals that the beast (Antichrist) is in cohorts with a "prostitute" ... who is this prostitute? It is the one world religion that will emerge. It will be the marriage of religion and politics, producing a terrible combination of powerful corruption. This corrupt religious system covers the whole planet ... the meaning of the phrase "who sits on many waters" ... "waters" being a reference to humanity or nations ... the "sea of humanity."

Politics and religion never mix well!

The tribulation period will NOT be without lots of religion, but it will be a false religion! It will be religion

USED to control people, to give power to rulers. Christ gives power to individuals to change their hearts. He never used His power on earth to control the nation of Rome; rather, Jesus refused to make His teachings political ... He saved tax collectors, Pharisees, prostitutes, demon-possessed individuals, the lame, the dumb, zealots, Roman soldiers, fishermen, farmers, Jews, Gentiles, Greeks, Romans, women, children, men, etc. Jesus wasn't interested in political power. He was interested in God's power to change the heart and life.

The Antichrist will use religion to support his goals ... he will no doubt appear quite religious. It will be a necessary but uncomfortable marriage for him to accomplish his tasks ... and once he has done so and has complete power, he will discard this one world religion and destroy it! Revelation 17:16 tells us: "The beast and the ten horns you saw will hate the prostitute. They will bring her to ruin and leave her naked; they will eat her flesh and burn her with fire." Never has politicizing religion been positive ... even our relatively recent history has shown this. Hitler mixed his political goals by wedding them to religious principles. True religion is a personal relationship with Jesus Christ, not a political relationship.

It is clear that the Antichrist will effectively use

religion to move the masses to follow him and his agenda. This false church will be a counterfeit Christianity, complete with great miracles and the expectation of complete commitment. God is still in control, even with a false worldwide religion in place. God's purposes will not be destroyed by Satan or man's religious efforts. Though this latter-day religious system will corrupt the world, it will lose in the end. While it is clear that religion will play a large role in the support of the Antichrist, it will fail to change the world positively! Though successful for a time, all religions will fail ... only the rule of Christ will continue into eternity!

Finally, the day of collapse will come for evil ... Satan will lose — he is even now a loser! There will be a total collapse of Satan's kingdom. This is the meaning here: "Fallen! Fallen is Babylon the Great! She has become a home for demons and a haunt for every evil spirit, a haunt for every unclean and detestable bird." Evil's apparent victory ends ... in a total collapse.

Full judgment will come upon all evil and evil doers ... they will not escape. God does not forget evil or those who are evil doers, and He will bring judgment. Notice in Revelation 18:5: "For her sins are piled up to heaven, and God has remembered her crimes." All those who have conquered nations will see their powers fail, their rule ended, and only the kingdom of God will last!

The collapse of Satan's kingdom will be so complete that it will astonish the world ... those whose gods were gold and silver will simply mourn their financial losses, yet the greatest loss will be their souls! The phrases used here: "In one hour your doom has come!" and "In one hour she has been brought to ruin!" clearly indicate the quickness with which the end will come. Evil's reign will be short-lived in the annals of eternity.

The suddenness of the destruction is shown by the image John uses of a millstone being suddenly thrust into the sea ... indicating a quick end! All normal activities will cease. Evil thought it could prosper forever, that God would not win ... but evil comes to an end quickly and totally, and with it all the prosperity of the wicked.

We must not envy those who get rich by deceit, for there WILL BE a final judgment that will end their prosperity ... it will be the day of victory for the righteous!

The day of evil's rule is coming to an end. What a glorious day it will be for the saints, and what a horrible day it will be for sinners! Where will you be on that day? Why not be on the winning side NOW?

Though we often feel frustrated that evil sometimes goes unpunished and good seems unrewarded, there is coming a day when evil will receive its just deserts and the righteous will rejoice and be rewarded. Don't lose heart in your service for God. He will not let evil triumph or escape judgment.

Living for God is NOT in vain! In Christ you are on the winning side ... stand firm in faith!

The Celebration

Revelation 19:1-21

After this I heard what seemed to be the loud voice of a great multitude in heaven, crying out,

"Hallelujah! Salvation and glory and power belong to our God, for his judgments are true and just; for he has judged the great prostitute who corrupted the earth with her immorality, and has avenged on her the blood of his servants."

Once more they cried out, "Hallelujah! The smoke from her goes up forever and ever."

And the twenty-four elders and the four living creatures fell down and worshiped God who was seated on the throne, saying, "Amen. Hallelujah!" And from the throne came a voice saying,

"Praise our God, all you his servants, you who fear him, small and great."

Then I heard what seemed to be the voice of a great multitude, like the roar of many waters and like the sound of mighty peals of thunder, crying out, "Hallelujah! For the Lord our God the Almighty reigns. Let us rejoice and exult and give him the glory, for the marriage of the Lamb has come, and his Bride has made herself ready; it was granted her to clothe herself with fine linen, bright and pure"—

for the fine linen is the righteous deeds of the saints.

And the angel said to me, "Write this: Blessed are those who are invited to the marriage supper of the Lamb." And he said to me, "These are the true words of God." Then I fell down at his feet to worship him, but he said to me, "You must not do that! I am a fellow servant with you and your brothers who hold to the testimony of Jesus. Worship God." For the testimony of Jesus is the spirit of prophecy.

Then I saw heaven opened, and behold, a white horse! The one sitting on it is called Faithful and True, and in righteousness he judges and makes war. His eyes are like a flame of fire, and on his head are many diadems, and he has a name written that no one knows but himself. He is clothed in a robe dipped in blood, and the name by which he is called is The Word of God. And the armies of heaven, arrayed in fine linen, white and pure, were following him on white horses. From his mouth comes a sharp sword with which to strike down the nations, and he will rule them with a rod of iron. He will tread the winepress of the fury of the wrath of God the Almighty. On his robe and on his thigh he has a name written, King of kings and Lord of lords.

Then I saw an angel standing in the sun, and with a loud voice he called to all the birds that fly directly overhead, "Come, gather for the great supper of God, to eat the flesh of kings, the flesh of captains, the flesh of mighty men, the flesh of horses and their riders, and the flesh of all men, both free and slave, both small and great." And I saw the beast and the kings of the earth with their armies gathered to make war against him who was sitting on the horse and against his army. And the beast was captured, and with it the false prophet who in its presence had done the signs by which he deceived those who had received the mark of the beast and those who worshiped its image. These two were thrown alive into the lake of fire that burns with sulfur. And the rest were slain by the sword that came from the mouth of him who was sitting on the horse, and all the birds were gorged with their flesh.

There is coming a day when Christians will have a far greater reason to celebrate than any previous event in history! Simply put, Jesus is coming again! John has spent considerable space in the book of Revelation telling us about the horrendous events of the tribulation on earth, but here he turns the focus to the greatest celebration of all time for Christians, the second coming of Jesus Christ and the final victory over sin and Satan.

If you think you have been in a great celebration before, you "ain't seen nothing yet!" All the things you do throughout your lifetime to prepare for Christ's coming won't be in vain ... they will pay off one day, big time! Don't be afraid to prepare for the day of the Lord's coming ... sometime in the future, you will be glad you did!

The Bible clearly teaches that Jesus is coming again. It will be a day of great celebration for believers of all ages, and a day of terror for those who have rejected Christ in this life, so accept Christ and join in the celebration!

Evil's day will come to an end, and the power of Satan will be destroyed! It isn't always easy to deal with the way evil works, especially when it at times seems to triumph, but those days are coming to an end. This is not just a "pie in the sky" theology, it is a real hope, an actual day when Christ will end the influence of evil over mankind.

This life isn't all there is. We are born for eternity ... the only question is where we will spend it. Those who have received Christ will receive all the rewards that Christ has promised, including eternal life with Him. For those who reject the Savior, they are on their own ... a terrible place to be in eternity. Some have thought that this will be the worst part about hell, that we will be left to ourselves in darkness forever, separated from God. So many will be shocked at death to discover that they are still alive ... do you really want to gamble away that moment by rejecting Christ today?

It would have been a strange thing indeed if God had made us to exist only for a short spot of time. He made Adam to be an eternal living being, and although sin distorted what he was, Christ's death made possible our restoration with God so that our eternal life can still be what He intended it to be. You can be on the front seat of the greatest celebration of all time ... no wonder the roar of the crowd in heaven was "Hallelujah!" This word "hallelujah" is said four times in the chapter, and it is the only passage in the entire New Testament where it is used!

The message is clear as John writes here … Christians have a great day of celebration coming … be ready for it!

So often the New Testament writers equated the church with the image of a bride, with Christ as the bridegroom. What a great image! Marriage is the result of great love between a bridegroom and bride … it is one of the greatest days between lovers. What a great image for the church … Christ's undying love for His church will bring Him back to get us … for now we enjoy engagement, but the wedding day is coming when we will be united to Christ forever.

Jesus has changed this planet already … so much of what the world is today has been deeply influenced by Jesus Christ … even for those who do not believe in Him, their world today would not exist if it hadn't been for Christ! So why ignore the greatest moment in history … when Christ comes for His church and the greatest marriage and celebration of all time takes place? Don't be on the outside looking in. You can be a participant by accepting Christ as your Lord.

What a contrast the picture of the church is here to the "prostitute" church John talked about in 17:1, 4 … The false church was called a "prostitute" dressed in scarlet and purple, decked with jewels in 17:1, 4. The church here is simply said to be dressed in fine white linen, bright and clean ... the picture of purity and waiting for her bride, Jesus Christ.

This will be one marriage you won't want to miss!! John says there will be a great marriage supper, and Christ says, "Blessed are those who are invited to the wedding supper of the Lamb!" This will be the wedding celebration of all time ... don't be left out. The invitation was given to John in John 3:16 ... "Whosoever believes in Him shall not perish but have everlasting life." You have already received the invitation ... have you responded yet, so that you will be there?

From the wedding scene, John now shifts to what follows the wedding ... the moment of destroying Satan's schemes on earth. John sees heaven open, and Christ sits on a white horse with an army of saints behind Him ready for conquest. Christ is wearing "many crowns" ... He alone is "King of Kings, Lord of Lords." The crown of thorns has been replaced now by many crowns, for there is no power greater than Christ's! Jesus at His second coming will be wearing many crowns, the only ruler over all.

There will be another feast to attend besides the marriage supper of the Lamb ... but it will be a horrible feast! Christ will call for the birds of the air to come and feast on the bodies of the wicked which He will destroy by the word of His mouth! Finally, the wicked will receive their just rewards. This is, after all, the fulfillment of what sinners were warned about in the Bible ... Paul did say in Romans that the "wages of sin is death."

Yes, you can get away with sin for now ... but there is a judgment day coming when all sin will be punished. Why be a part of this horrible feast when you can be at the marriage supper of the Lamb instead? There is such a contrast between the two feasts mentioned by John, and the amazing thing is that we have the option to choose which one we will be at. Which invitation will you accept?

Christ comes with a robe dipped in blood ... but not the blood of others. It is His own blood which He shed for us, so our robes can be clean and spotless. Only those with clean robes were allowed at marriage suppers ... guests were often given white robes when they arrived. Christ clothes us with His own right-eousness, and His blood washes us clean.

Without this robe of righteousness, there is no entrance to the marriage supper of the Lamb ... the only feast will be for the birds, and it will be the wicked that are destroyed. You can guarantee your entrance to the marriage supper of the Lamb by accepting Christ's invitation to be cleansed by His blood. This was the purpose for Christ's death on Calvary.

Christ now deals with the arrogant Antichrist and false prophet that deceived the world and led so many down paths of wickedness. The two of them are captured by Christ and thrown into the "fiery lake of burning sulfur." They will be sent there alone for 1,000 years ... their end is what they deserve! The rest of the wicked will die and remain in their graves until the end of the millennial reign of Christ, then they will be raised and judged and sent to outer darkness forever.

Sin causes arrogance and pride ... rejecting the very God who can save. It is a tragic thing to see how hard the sinful heart can be ... to ignore God's salvation is foolish. Without Christ in your life you will not see God. How foolish to trade a few years of independence and sinful pleasures and miss heaven. It would indeed be a foolish trade. Christ brings us life, joyful and full life ... it is not a life of "no fun;" it is full of great joy ... joy that will become an even greater joy at His coming. We need not fear Satan and sin if we have Christ in our hearts ... He will conquer all wickedness and reward all those who live for Him.

The end of evildoers is coming ... and the kingdom of God will be manifest in all its fullness. All those who live for Christ now will rule with Christ then. Everyone likes to be on the winning team. How about you ... have you joined the conqueror of all times? Jesus Christ can lock in your seat at the marriage supper of the Lamb. Receive His invitation today!

Christ is coming again ... are you ready if it happens today, tomorrow ... or soon?

The church is often called the "bride of Christ," and one day we will celebrate the marriage of the bride with the Lamb of God. That day will be a great celebration for all believers! For the wicked, however, it will be a time of defeat and eternal loss. Today, we have a choice, to be the bride of Christ or the rejected.

Are you ready for the second coming of Christ? Will you be celebrating His coming?

The Conclusion

Revelation 20:1-22:6; Isaiah 65:17-25

Then I saw an angel coming down from heaven, holding in his hand the key to the bottomless pit and a great chain. And he seized the dragon, that ancient serpent, who is the devil and Satan, and bound him for a thousand years, and threw him into the pit, and shut it and sealed it over him, so that he might not deceive the nations any longer, until the thousand years were ended. After that he must be released for a little while.

Then I saw thrones, and seated on them were those to whom the authority to judge was committed. Also I saw the souls of those who had been beheaded for the testimony of Jesus and for the word of God, and those who had not worshiped the beast or its image and had not received its mark on their foreheads or their hands. They came

to life and reigned with Christ for a thousand years.
The rest of the dead did not come to life until the
thousand years were ended. This is the first
resurrection. Blessed and holy is the one who
shares in the first resurrection! Over such the
second death has no power, but they will be priests
of God and of Christ, and they will reign with him
for a thousand years.

And when the thousand years are ended, Satan will
be released from his prison and will come out to
deceive the nations that are at the four corners of
the earth, Gog and Magog, to gather them for
battle; their number is like the sand of the sea. And
they marched up over the broad plain of the earth
and surrounded the camp of the saints and the
beloved city, but fire came down from heaven and
consumed them, and the devil who had deceived
them was thrown into the lake of fire and sulfur
where the beast and the false prophet were, and
they will be tormented day and night forever and
ever.

Then I saw a great white throne and him who was
seated on it. From his presence earth and sky fled
away, and no place was found for them. And I saw
the dead, great and small, standing before the
throne, and books were opened. Then another
book was opened, which is the book of life. And the
dead were judged by what was written in the

books, according to what they had done. And the sea gave up the dead who were in it, Death and Hades gave up the dead who were in them, and they were judged, each one of them, according to what they had done. Then Death and Hades were thrown into the lake of fire. This is the second death, the lake of fire. And if anyone's name was not found written in the book of life, he was thrown into the lake of fire.

Then I saw a new heaven and a new earth, for the first heaven and the first earth had passed away, and the sea was no more. And I saw the holy city, new Jerusalem, coming down out of heaven from God, prepared as a bride adorned for her husband. And I heard a loud voice from the throne saying, "Behold, the dwelling place of God is with man. He will dwell with them, and they will be his people, and God himself will be with them as their God. He will wipe away every tear from their eyes, and death shall be no more, neither shall there be mourning, nor crying, nor pain anymore, for the former things have passed away."

And he who was seated on the throne said, "Behold, I am making all things new." Also he said, "Write this down, for these words are trustworthy and true." And he said to me, "It is done! I am the Alpha and the Omega, the beginning and the end. To the thirsty I will give from the spring of the *water of life without payment. The one who conquers will have this heritage, and I will be his God and he will be my son. But as for the cowardly, the faithless, the detestable, as for murderers, the sexually immoral, sorcerers, idolaters, and all liars, their portion will be in the lake that burns with fire and sulfur, which is the second death."*

Then came one of the seven angels who had the seven bowls full of the seven last plagues and spoke to me, saying, "Come, I will show you the Bride, the wife of the Lamb." And he carried me away in the Spirit to a great, high mountain, and showed me the holy city Jerusalem coming down out of heaven from God, having the glory of God, its radiance like a most rare jewel, like a jasper, clear as crystal. It had a great, high wall, with twelve gates, and at the gates twelve angels, and on the gates the names of the twelve tribes of the sons of Israel were inscribed— on the east three gates, on the north three gates, on the south three gates, and on the west three gates. And the wall of the city had twelve foundations, and on them were the twelve names of the twelve apostles of the Lamb.

And the one who spoke with me had a measuring rod of gold to measure the city and its gates and walls. The city lies foursquare, its length the same as its width. And he measured the city with his rod,

12,000 stadia. Its length and width and height are equal. He also measured its wall, 144 cubits by human measurement, which is also an angel's measurement. The wall was built of jasper, while the city was pure gold, like clear glass. The foundations of the wall of the city were adorned with every kind of jewel. The first was jasper, the second sapphire, the third agate, the fourth emerald, the fifth onyx, the sixth carnelian, the seventh chrysolite, the eighth beryl, the ninth topaz, the tenth chrysoprase, the eleventh jacinth, the twelfth amethyst. And the twelve gates were twelve pearls, each of the gates made of a single pearl, and the street of the city was pure gold, like transparent glass.

And I saw no temple in the city, for its temple is the Lord God the Almighty and the Lamb. And the city has no need of sun or moon to shine on it, for the glory of God gives it light, and its lamp is the Lamb. By its light will the nations walk, and the kings of the earth will bring their glory into it, and its gates will never be shut by day—and there will be no night there. They will bring into it the glory and the honor of the nations. But nothing unclean will ever enter it, nor anyone who does what is detestable or false, but only those who are written in the Lamb's book of life.

Then the angel showed me the river of the water of

life, bright as crystal, flowing from the throne of God and of the Lamb through the middle of the street of the city; also, on either side of the river, the tree of life with its twelve kinds of fruit, yielding its fruit each month. The leaves of the tree were for the healing of the nations. No longer will there be anything accursed, but the throne of God and of the Lamb will be in it, and his servants will worship him. They will see his face, and his name will be on their foreheads. And night will be no more. They will need no light of lamp or sun, for the Lord God will be their light, and they will reign forever and ever.

And he said to me, "These words are trustworthy and true. And the Lord, the God of the spirits of the prophets, has sent his angel to show his servants what must soon take place."

"For behold, I create new heavens and a new earth, and the former things shall not be remembered or come into mind. But be glad and rejoice forever in that which I create; for behold, I create Jerusalem to be a joy, and her people to be a gladness. I will rejoice in Jerusalem and be glad in my people; no more shall be heard in it the sound of weeping and the cry of distress. No more shall there be in it an infant who lives but a few days, or an old man who does not fill out his days, for the young man shall die a hundred years old, and the

sinner a hundred years old shall be accursed. They shall build houses and inhabit them; they shall plant vineyards and eat their fruit. They shall not build and another inhabit; they shall not plant and another eat; for like the days of a tree shall the days of my people be, and my chosen shall long enjoy the work of their hands. They shall not labor in vain or bear children for calamity, for they shall be the offspring of the blessed of the Lord, and their descendants with them.

"Before they call I will answer; while they are yet speaking I will hear. The wolf and the lamb shall graze together; the lion shall eat straw like the ox, and dust shall be the serpent's food. They shall not hurt or destroy in all my holy mountain," says the Lord.

The second coming of Jesus Christ will usher in a unique time in human history. Christ will physically rule and reign on the earth for 1,000 years. The Bible calls this the "millennial reign of Christ."

Politicians and rulers have said for a long time that the world would become paradise if everyone was free and had a job, if everyone was educated, if diseases and wars were wiped out. It has been man's belief that if we could achieve these goals, then crime would cease and peace would rule the world. WELL ... a day like this will come, but it won't be the result of political or financial success. It will be the power of Jesus Christ ruling and reigning over the earth after binding up Satan for 1,000 years.

The human dream will be realized, but only because Christ overcomes and binds up Satan. To be a part of this wonderful time of 1,000 years of prosperity, however, one must belong to Christ on this side of eternity so they can rule with Him on the other side of eternity. What kingdom do you belong to? The opportunity to experience the greatest kingdom on earth will only come to those who belong to the kingdom of heaven!

The Bible teaches us that Christ will return to establish an earthly kingdom of righteousness, where Satan will be bound, and the world will know the reality of the promises God made to Israel long ago for a righteous kingdom ruled by the son of David ... Jesus Christ Himself.

The first thing Jesus does when His second coming occurs is to capture Satan and have him bound by chains and thrown into the Abyss where he is locked away for 1,000 years. Satan will not be able to deceive humanity during this time. The power of evil will be severely restricted.

This 1,000-year reign of Christ on the earth will fulfill the promises God made to Abraham and the Israelites in the Old Testament, promises of a great kingdom where God would rule and Israel would be a nation of priests.

God never forgets or ignores His promises. So many of the hopes of the Jews in the Old Testament were wrapped up in this future kingdom, a time of great joy and peace, where the laws of nature reflected the presence of God and Satan was conquered. Such passages as Isaiah 65:17-25 show the anticipation of that future kingdom ... the one fulfilled here in Christ's millennial reign.

Satan and his followers are deceived by their pride right now ... they act as though God doesn't exist and they don't have to obey any spiritual truths ... they just do their own thing and don't worry about consequences. This is the tragedy of all sinners who reject Christ's offer of salvation. Sin makes one self-sufficient and arrogant, but there is coming a day when this pride will end, and it will be costly! If only sinners really knew what was coming, they might act differently today! Satan likes to keep his followers blind to the future, even as he himself stays blind to the future.

God, however, will never ignore His promises, and

He has promised over and over again that He will come and rule and reign over a kingdom of great beauty on the earth ... Christ will fulfill this and all the promises of God. As Isaiah 65:17-25 states, that millennial kingdom will be one of great joy, long lifespans, fulfillment and joy like the world has never seen before. With Satan locked up and away from mankind, the world will be set free from his influence ... but this doesn't mean that all sin is gone, for it still resides in the hearts of fallen men who survive the tribulation period and live on into the millennial reign of Christ.

All those who lived for Christ will be a part of this millennial reign of Christ. Citizenship is based on our relationship with Christ, not what political party we belonged to on earth or our connections with the right people. Those who lived for Christ will enjoy this kingdom in the future. Those whose lives have been touched by Christ will enjoy His presence and His kingdom rule in the future. All those who lived by kingdom principles on this side of eternity will participate in the future kingdom reality of Christ's rule. Those who rejected Christ's ways on earth will not participate in this future kingdom ... they lived for themselves here, and they will live with themselves in eternity ... away from God and His kingdom! It will be a tragic time for those who rejected Christ in this lifetime.

At the end of the 1,000 years, Satan is loosed for a short season. WHY? To allow all those who were born during this period to make the same choice all humans have had between following Christ or the devil. This will be short, and tragically there will be those who will turn away from God, even after living in a perfect environment and world for 1,000 years! This only goes to prove that giving everyone a job, good health care, and their own place won't wipe away the sinful heart. Only Christ can accomplish this!

Following this thousand years, God will cast Satan and all sinners into hell, and it will be removed forever from God's presence and His people. There is no escape from the lake of fire ... it is eternal hell. Today is the day of salvation. Don't neglect so great a gift!

Now God destroys all the old things, even the old universe as we know it.

God will create a new heavens and earth ... without sin, without Satan's presence, and without sinners ... only righteousness. With no defects in this universe, there will be no decline or decay, and everything will be permanent. God will restore man to Paradise, the real one! No more death, no more mourning, no more pain, no more sickness or sin!

Indeed, it will be paradise! This is what God intended for man all along. Turning away from God caused all the heartache the world has known since that day. What a wonderful future is in store for those who live for God!

The New Jerusalem will live up to its name unlike the old one! (Jerusalem means "Possession of Peace" or "Foundation of Peace.") It will be a beautiful place. The Bible even gives us its size: 12,000 stadia in three dimensions (approx. 1,380 miles in each direction). It has been estimated that if only 25% of this space was used for living quarters or dwellings it could accommodate 20 BILLION people, surely large enough to hold all of God's people down through the ages.

It will be the city of paradise that we could never imagine here on earth! It will be far better than any paradise here now! It will belong to God's people for eternity! It will be all that God wanted for us before we sinned in Eden. God's power will give us life forever. He who is the "Living Water" will fulfill all our needs throughout eternity. Our strength comes from Christ, not only now, but forever! This river of life flows from the throne of God for all to enjoy in the New Jerusalem.

Christ's power sustains us now and will in the future, too. Our life consists of Christ's power. He who resurrects us will keep us eternally. No other power on earth has been able to promise a city like this, the place of God's presence. Mankind has tried again and again to create paradise, but always with disastrous results! Man's efforts will never match God's! The only hope for paradise begins with Christ!

Forever is a long time! This is why it is so important that we make wise choices now. The blessings of God will last forever ... pleasures of sin only last for a short season. It is important that we choose wisely today, for tomorrow hinges on what we do today.

Even now we experience God's goodness in our lives, but this will be nothing compared to what God has in store for us. If we can get excited about God's blessings now, imagine what we will experience in the New Heavens and New Earth that are coming. No more separation from God. No more pain or sorrow of any kind, no more death, no more darkness, etc. This is much more than "pie in the sky" theology or escapism ... it is reality! There is nothing wrong with having hope in the future and looking forward to being with Christ in eternity. In fact, it often has very practical implications in the present ... for when we hope in the future, we live more circumspectly in the present, hardly the stuff of escapism!

Are you anticipating what God has in store for all

those who love Him and live for Him? You can be ready for it when it comes, no matter when it comes! Living for Christ now will guarantee your presence in His kingdom in eternity. You are going to live forever somewhere. Why not pick a great place like the New Jerusalem? The other option is a "dump!"

The tragic power of sin will one day fade away and be replaced by the glory of God's power and rule. The course we take tomorrow begins with the choice we make today. Knowing Christ will rule and reign forever, why not choose now to follow Him? God has great things in store for all those who love His appearing!

The Challenge

Revelation 22:7-21

"And behold, I am coming soon. Blessed is the one who keeps the words of the prophecy of this book."

I, John, am the one who heard and saw these things. And when I heard and saw them, I fell down to worship at the feet of the angel who showed them to me, but he said to me, "You must not do that! I am a fellow servant with you and your brothers the prophets, and with those who keep the words of this book. Worship God."

And he said to me, "Do not seal up the words of the prophecy of this book, for the time is near. Let the evildoer still do evil, and the filthy still be filthy, and the righteous still do right, and the holy still be holy."

"Behold, I am coming soon, bringing my

recompense with me, to repay each one for what he has done. I am the Alpha and the Omega, the first and the last, the beginning and the end."

Blessed are those who wash their robes, so that they may have the right to the tree of life and that they may enter the city by the gates. Outside are the dogs and sorcerers and the sexually immoral and murderers and idolaters, and everyone who loves and practices falsehood.

"I, Jesus, have sent my angel to testify to you about these things for the churches. I am the root and the descendant of David, the bright morning star."

The Spirit and the Bride say, "Come." And let the one who hears say, "Come." And let the one who is thirsty come; let the one who desires take the water of life without price.

I warn everyone who hears the words of the prophecy of this book: if anyone adds to them, God will add to him the plagues described in this book, and if anyone takes away from the words of the book of this prophecy, God will take away his share in the tree of life and in the holy city, which are described in this book.

He who testifies to these things says, "Surely I am coming soon." Amen. Come, Lord Jesus!

The grace of the Lord Jesus be with all. Amen.

It is interesting that the end of a book filled with so many ominous events should end with an invitation and prayer. The purpose of the book is not to depress the reader but to move the reader into a deep and loving relationship with Christ so that the future is bright and not dark.

The challenge then is clear, how do we get the message out ... because failure to do so will leave a lot of people heading for a godless eternity!

The Spirit of God concludes the Revelation of Jesus Christ as it began ... revealing Christ and His invitation to find real life. The book is NOT PRIMARILY the "Revelation of the FUTURE" as much as it is the "Revelation of JESUS CHRIST" — His person, His plans, His promise, His perfection ... and His desire to have as many join Him in eternity as possible! OUR CHALLENGE is to take HIS message to everyone and give them the opportunity to accept Christ and escape the godless eternity that is certain without Christ.

The Bible contains two challenges as we come to the end of the book. For believers, the challenge is to get the message out that Jesus is coming again and that people can be saved so they are ready for it; and for unbelievers, the challenge is to trust God rather than the progress and plans of man.

The revelation ends with a powerful promise: "Behold, I am coming soon!" It seems hard to believe it can be soon in light of all the things predicted and the wide perspective of events that John has recorded, but His coming is closer than we think. Don't be fooled into thinking that too much has yet to happen before He can come ... He IS coming SOON! The challenge in realizing that He is coming soon is for us to keep the words of this prophecy ... to be walking with God so we are ready for it when it happens! Every Christian should have the expectancy of Christ's return burning in their hearts ... it is clear the early church did.

It seems so odd that many modern "scholars" say that the book of Revelation is not prophetic but only full of metaphors on the history of the church's struggle in the past ... ironic because Jesus' own words here says it is PROPHECY! "Blessed is he who keeps the words of the prophecy in this book." Jesus' own words here proclaim the book prophetic, and it seems odd that anyone else would call it anything else! Why a prophetic book? So that we are looking forward in faith to a great future, staying faithful in the present, and grateful that our past won't condemn us!

John's reaction here gives us a clear message

about worship: DON'T worship anything BUT GOD HIMSELF! In a world that can draw us away from God to worship many other things, this is an important message. John's reaction to fall at the feet of this angel in light of the tremendous revelation he has just received shows the power of misguided emotions. Surely John was very emotional at this moment and his guard was down as he fell to worship this angel rather than Jesus ... the angel stops him with a direct order: "DO NOT DO IT!" This is good advice about getting off track in our worship with anything else except Christ. Simply put, "DO NOT DO IT."

Mankind cannot ignore the important message of Revelation ... today, Jesus is your savior, but if you ignore that message, tomorrow, He will be your judge!

Jesus' words here, "Behold I am coming soon!" ... "my reward is with me ..." and "blessed are those who have washed their robes ..." are intended to empha- size the importance of being "READY!" — prepared!

Jesus has given this word so that we are not caught off guard. Are you ready?

An interesting statement is made here: "The Spirit AND the bride say, 'COME!'" (emphasis mine) Getting the message out is a partnership of both the Spirit of God and the church of Jesus Christ. We are to work together to give the invitation!

We CANNOT invite people to Christ WITHOUT the Spirit, and the Spirit works through Christ's church! No believer should be independent from the church! We are working together with God's Spirit!

This is a powerful truth ... the Spirit and the bride have the SAME passion! No church is a New Testament church that doesn't anticipate the return of Christ! No Spirit-filled church is going to be apathetic about the second coming of Jesus Christ! If the SPIRIT AND the BRIDE say "COME!" ... and it is followed with an exclamation mark in the verse ... then it cannot be that the church is indifferent to this truth.

This partnership is all about INVITATION ... "COME!" Together we are strong, alone we are weak. We speak and feel the same thing. The Spirit and the bride should have one voice ... an invitation to "COME!" The invitation is good for ALL ... notice how many times the word "COME" is used in this verse! The call is out to everyone! God "is not willing that any should perish, but all COME" ...

If people keep hearing that Jesus is coming, and if they keep hearing the invitation to "COME," then some will respond! But our failure to talk about Christ's coming and the invitation to come will result in people not even being aware of their eternal destination.

Likewise, if we constantly talk about Jesus' coming and invite people to come to Christ, they are more likely to. They will think more and more about it. A church that expects Christ's return and speaks about it will tend to have a more serious approach to evangelizing the lost ... they know the future will soon be here! A true mindset of Jesus' soon coming creates a passion about the lost.

Jesus throws the net wide for who can come ... "... whoever wishes, let him take the free gift ..."

No one is to alter the message ... neither add to it nor take away from the prophecy of this book! There are strong warnings here to those who would alter the message in any way! We have a clear message already ... we just need to be faithful to preach it!

It is critical that we preach the Word ... and give the call to come to Christ. The world doesn't realize what's coming, and without the Word of God, they may never know the danger they are in! And that is why there are warnings against CHANGING the message, to neither add nor delete anything from it ... the outcome is too important. We cannot mess with the message! The message of salvation is critical for a person's future happiness, but if they don't hear it, they won't know this.

The message becomes diluted when men start taking out of God's Word parts they don't think are breathed by the Spirit, or add things that aren't there ... we are only safe with the message the way it was delivered by God, without alterations!

Preach the message, keep it pure, watch its power!

The final two verses of the Bible and the book of Revelation contain both a promise and a prayer. OUR PROMISE: "Yes, I am coming soon." OUR PRAYER: "Amen. Come, Lord Jesus. The grace of the Lord Jesus be with God's people. Amen."

The promise promotes the prayer ... so we must be careful not to lose sight of the promise or fail to take it seriously! It is too easy to allow ourselves to become so EARTHLY MINDED that we are no HEAVENLY GOOD! (How's that for a twist!?) If we become sidetracked from this great truth of Jesus' coming, we will lose our passion for the lost!

We cannot afford the distractions from the message or the mission. God's grace is the prayer John offers for the saints, a wonderful gift! While we wait for Christ's return, we exist within His grace.

The bottom line is this: Christ is coming SOON, and all His children should pray, "AMEN, Come, Lord

Jesus." Is this your prayer? Are you ready? You can be!

The close of the book of Revelation is a fitting challenge to two groups — to believers, the challenge of being faithful to reach the lost; and to the unbeliever, to trust in Christ before it is too late. Jesus promised He was coming soon ... and to God who says that a thousand years to man is but one day to Him, it is VERY soon until He comes. Are you ready for Christ's coming? It could be today!

About Tim R. Barker

Reverend Tim R. Barker is the Superintendent of the South Texas District of the Assemblies of God which is headquartered in Houston, Texas.

He is a graduate of Southwestern Assemblies of God University, with a Bachelor of Science degree in General Ministries/Biblical Studies, with a minor in music. He also received a Master of Arts in Practical Theology from SAGU and received his Doctorate of Ministry Degree from West Coast Seminary.

Reverend Barker was ordained by the Assemblies of God in 1989. He began his ministry in the South Texas District in 1984 as youth & music minister and continued his ministry as Pastor, Executive Presbyter (2006 – 2009) and Executive Secretary-Treasurer (2009 – 2011) in the South Texas District, where he served until his election as the South Texas District Superintendent in 2011.

By virtue of his district office, Reverend Barker is a member of the District's Executive Presbytery and the General Presbytery of the General Council of the Assemblies of God, Springfield, Missouri. He is a member of the Executive Board of Regents for Southwestern Assemblies of God University, Waxahachie, Texas and SAGU-American Indian College, Phoenix, Arizona. He is a member of the Board of Directors of Pleasant Hills Children's Home, Fairfield, Texas, as well as numerous other boards and committees.

Reverend Barker and his wife, Jill, married in 1983, have been blessed with two daughters. Jordin and her husband, Stancle Williams, who serves as the South Texas District Youth Director. Abrielle and her husband, Nolan McLaughlin, are church planters of Motion Church in San Antonio. The Barkers have four grandchildren, Braylen, Emory and Landon Williams and Kingston McLaughlin.

His unique style of pulpit ministry and musical background challenges the body of Christ, with an appeal that reaches the generations.

Contact Tim

Pastor Tim would love to hear from you. You can reach him at www.TimBarker.ag.

Click on Ask Pastor Tim for more information.

Made in the USA
Monee, IL
16 February 2022